On the Beach

NEVIL SHUTE

Level 4

Retold by G. C. Thornley
Series Editors: Andy Hopkins and Jocelyn Potter

Pearson Education Limited
Edinburgh Gate, Harlow,
Essex CM20 2JE, England
and Associated Companies throughout the world.

ISBN: 978-1-4058-8228-6

First published in the Longman Structural Readers Series 1972
in association with William Heinemann Ltd
This adaptation first published by Addison Wesley Longman Ltd
in the Longman Fiction Series 1996
First published by Penguin Books Ltd 1999
This edition first published by Pearson Education Ltd 2008

10

Original © by the Trustees of the Estate of the late Nevil Shute Norway 1957
This edition copyright © Penguin Books Ltd 1999
Illustrations by Alistair Adams

Typeset by Graphicraft Ltd, Hong Kong
Set in 11/14pt Bembo
Printed in China
SWTC/10

*All rights reserved; no part of this publication may be reproduced, stored
in a retrieval system, or transmitted in any form or by any means,
electronic, mechanical, photocopying, recording or otherwise, without the
prior written permission of the Publishers.*

Published by Pearson Education Ltd

Every effort has been made to trace the copyright holders and we apologise in advance
for any unintentional omissions. We would be pleased to insert the appropriate
acknowledgement in any subsequent edition of this publication.

For a complete list of the titles available in the Pearson English Readers series, please
visit www.pearsonenglishreaders.com. Alternatively, write to your local Pearson Education
office or to Pearson English Readers Marketing Department, Pearson Education,
Edinburgh Gate, Harlow, Essex CM20 2JE, England.

Contents

		page
Introduction		v
Chapter 1	A New Appointment	1
Chapter 2	Preparing to Leave	23
Chapter 3	The First Journey	33
Chapter 4	Dreams and Reality	47
Chapter 5	Testing Relationships	63
Chapter 6	Journey to the Pacific	74
Chapter 7	A Time of Rest	92
Chapter 8	Last Pleasures	101
Chapter 9	The End of It All	110
Activities		119

Introduction

'I won't accept it,' she cried. 'Nobody ever dropped a cobalt bomb in the south, or any other kind of bomb. We didn't do anything. Why must we die because other countries wanted a war? They're fifteen or sixteen thousand kilometres away from us. And we have to die. It's not fair.'

'It isn't fair,' he said, 'but it's coming.'

On the Beach is about a subject that many writers would be too afraid to discuss. It tells of the terrible effects of a nuclear war. There has been a war between the northern countries of the world and everyone there is dead. But now the winds are carrying radioactive dust all around the world. One by one, the countries of the south are also dying. In the end, only Australia and New Zealand are free from the radiation. But everyone there knows that in a few months it will reach them. Then they will all become sick and die. What can these last few people do? Some continue working; some of them try to enjoy their last few months. Some make new friends, although they know it will be for only a short time.

This book first appeared in 1957. At that time many people in the world were very frightened of nuclear bombs and radiation. The first nuclear bombs were invented during the Second World War. After nuclear bombs were dropped on Hiroshima and Nagasaki in Japan, the world knew the power of these new, terrible bombs. Nobody had seen anything like them before. 70,000 people died immediately, and thousands died later from burns and from radioactive dust in the air.

Over the next ten years, the US and the USSR made more and bigger bombs. These two great powers were afraid that one of them might attack and destroy the other. Soon there were enough nuclear bombs in the world to kill everybody on Earth. And still they and a few other countries continued making bigger and more powerful bombs.

Writers wrote many stories about nuclear wars. In these stories, wars sometimes begin by accident. A person might be mad, 'push the red button' and cause the end of the world. Many films were made on the subject – serious films and even amusing ones. More countries made nuclear bombs. Everybody was waiting for a war to start.

Then in April, 1986, there was a serious accident in a nuclear power station at Chernobyl in Ukraine. Radiation from the accident seriously affected 6.6 million people. It travelled in the wind and the rain over large areas of Ukraine and Russia, and into east, west and northern Europe. Many people died; many more became sick from the radiation. People all over the world saw that one nuclear accident could spread radiation over a large area. They realized that even a few nuclear bombs would destroy not only the enemy country, but many other countries too. Nothing could stop the spread of the radiation.

Nevil Shute's book was different from other stories. Shute was not very interested in the causes of the nuclear war. In his book, the war has ended. In most countries in the world, people are already dead. In a nuclear war, Shute is telling us, there are no winners – only losers. But he did not live to see the end of the Cold War or the fall of the Berlin wall. He died in 1960, only three years after this book was finished.

Nevil Shute Norway was born in Ealing, London, in 1899. He served as a pilot during the First World War and then studied at Oxford University. He worked as an engineer at Howden Airship Works. He also worked for the Airship Guarantee Company during the building of the airship R100 and twice flew across the Atlantic in it. He started and later ran an aircraft factory called Airspeed. During the Second World War he served in a department of the Navy which was responsible for new inventions for war, but he gave up this work in 1945, at the age of forty-six, and became a full-time writer.

Soon after the war, in 1950, Shute and his family made their home in Australia. They lived on a farm at Langwarran, Victoria. Shute enjoyed life in Australia and became very fond of the people there. His later stories are about Australian people and places. He wrote more than twenty exciting adventure stories.

Many of his stories have appeared as films. Stanley Kramer's film of *On the Beach* came out in 1959. It starred Gregory Peck as Dwight Towers and Ava Gardner as Moira Davidson. It was the first full-length American film to be shown in Moscow and its strong message against nuclear bombs had a powerful effect in both east and west. At first the film was not a success in the United States. People thought it showed a weak attitude towards Russian power. The Pentagon refused to lend the film-makers a nuclear submarine, and newspapers said that its message against war was an invitation to the Russians to rule the world.

But slowly the message of the story was understood and accepted by more and more people. Groups of people in Europe and the US began to speak out against nuclear defences and the Cold War. These groups grew bigger and stronger through the years, and were finally strong enough to affect the views of politicians.

But year after year, more and more countries are making or buying nuclear bombs for their 'defence'. In *On the Beach*, Shute suggests that the war was begun by a small country, not one of the big powers. One day, a crazy, stupid leader of a small country might try to prove to his people that he is a proud, strong man by attacking an enemy country with a nuclear bomb. Then the next world war could begin in hours.

This book still has a message for everyone, today and always.

Chapter 1   A New Appointment

Lieutenant-Commander Peter Holmes, of the Royal Australian Navy, woke early. He lay half asleep for a time and watched the first light of the Australian sun on the window. The position of the sun showed that it was nearly five o'clock. Very soon the light would wake his baby daughter, Jennifer. There was no need to get up until that happened.

He woke happy, and he was not sure why. Then he remembered the date. This was Thursday, 27th December. Today he had to go to the Navy Department in Melbourne. He had to be there at eleven o'clock and he was hoping to receive a new appointment. If he got it, it would be his first work for five months. He hoped that he would be sent to sea again. He liked the sea better than a job on land.

He was happy because he would have work to do. He had not had any work since the Navy made him a Lieutenant-Commander. That was in August, and he had almost lost hope of working again. But the Navy Office had paid him during these months, and he was grateful for that.

His wife Mary woke and asked him the time. He kissed her and left the room to make some tea.

'It's a beautiful morning again,' he said when he came back.

'You're going to Melbourne today, aren't you?' she said. 'I think I'll stay at home. I can sit under the trees. It's going to be a hot day. Shall we meet this afternoon at the club? About four o'clock? We could have a swim there.'

They had a small car in the garage. Since the short war had ended, they had never used it. It had been in the garage for a year now. But Peter Holmes was a clever man with his hands. He had built a cart with two wheels that he pulled behind the car. Both

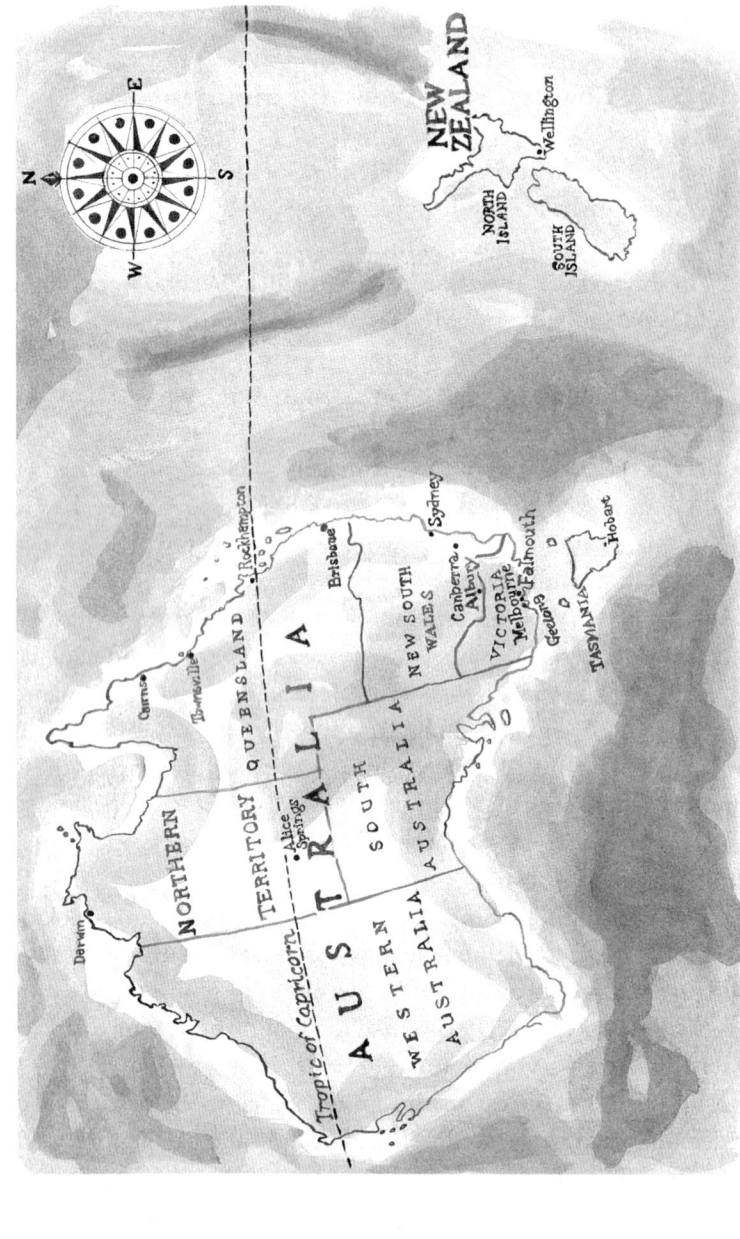

Mary and he had bicycles. He had fixed metal ties to the bicycles so that either he or she could use their bicycle to pull the cart. It could carry their daughter Jennifer or the shopping. Their main difficulty was the long hill up from Falmouth.

'A swim at the club isn't a bad idea,' he agreed. 'I'll take my bicycle and leave it at the station.'

'Yes. Take your bicycle. What train have you got to catch?'

'The five past nine.' He drank some tea and looked at his watch. 'I'll go and get the milk as soon as I've drunk this.'

He dressed and went out. They lived on the ground floor of an old house. It stood on the hill above the town. In his share of the building he had the garage and a good part of the garden. The car in the garage was a Morris. The Morris was his first car and he had had it when he met Mary.

He and Mary were married before the war. After the war started, he sailed away in the warship *Anzac*. They had expected that it would be a long war, but it did not last long. It quickly spread over the whole of the northern world, and there were a lot of explosions in different places. It died away with the last terrible explosion on the thirty-seventh day. At the end of the third month he had returned to Williamstown and then to his wife Mary and his Morris car.

The car had a little petrol in it. He bought some more and used it. But then Australians began to realize that all their oil came from the north.

He pulled the cart on to the grass near the house. He fixed it to his bicycle and rode away. He had to go six kilometres to get the milk. There were not many cars in use now in Australia; there was no petrol. So milk was never brought to the houses. He or Mary always went for it and carried it home in the cart.

There was not much traffic on the road. He passed something that had once been a car; but now the engine had gone, and the old car was pulled by a horse. He also passed two men on horses.

He did not want a horse for himself. Horses were sometimes ill, and they cost a lot of money now. Some of them cost a thousand pounds or more.

He reached the farm in half an hour and found the farmer immediately.

'Good morning, Mr Paul,' said the Lieutenant-Commander. 'How are you today?'

'Good,' was the reply. The farmer filled his milk can. 'How are you today? Is everything all right with you?'

'Yes, thanks. I've got to go to Melbourne. I have an appointment at the Navy Department. I think they've got a job for me.'

'That'll be a good thing,' the farmer said.

'Yes. If I have to go away to sea it'll be difficult, but Mary can come for the milk twice a week. She'll bring the money.'

The farmer said, 'You don't have to worry about the money until you come back. I've got more milk than the pigs need, even in this dry weather. I threw some away last night. I should get some more pigs, perhaps, but I'm not sure about the future.'

He stood in silence for a moment. Then he spoke again. 'Won't it be difficult for your wife? What will she do with Jennifer when she comes here?'

'She'll bring Jennifer too, perhaps, in the cart.'

'Not very easy, that!' The farmer walked away and looked closely at the cart.

'That's a good cart,' he said. 'I never saw a better one. You made it yourself, didn't you?'

'That's right,' said Peter.

'Where did you get the wheels, if I may ask?'

'They came off old bicycles. I got them in Elizabeth Street.'

'Could you find two for me?'

'I could try,' Peter said. 'They're better than the little wheels. They're easier to pull. But there aren't many now.'

'I was telling my wife about wheels,' the farmer said slowly. 'If I had a little cart like that, it would be useful. I could make it like a chair for the wife, fix it behind the bicycle and take her into Falmouth. She could go to the shops. It's very lonely for a woman in this place. It's not like before the war. She could take the car and reach the town in twenty minutes in those days, but now the horse and cart takes three and a half hours there and three and a half hours back. That's seven hours for travelling alone. That's a very long time. She tried to learn to ride the bicycle, but she'll never do it, not at her age. But if I had a cart, I could take her into Falmouth. We could go twice a week, and we could take the milk to Mrs Holmes at the same time.'

He paused. 'I want to do that for her. The radio says that we haven't got long now.'

'I'll have a look in town,' said Peter. 'You're able to pay a good price for the wheels?'

'Yes. But I want good tyres on them. Good tyres, that's the main thing. Like yours. But you'll have to go to a lot of shops.'

'I'll go by streetcar,' said Peter. 'Thank God for the coal.'

'How do they get the coal out? Do they dig it out with machines?'

'Yes. And then it's used to make electricity for the streetcars.'

'Where do they get the oil for the machines?'

'They make it from coal, but it costs a lot of money.'

Peter took the milk cans and put them in the cart. Then he started for home. It was half past six when he arrived.

He had a bath and put on his uniform. Then he ate his breakfast and rode his bicycle down the hill. Some horses were standing near the station. Cars used to stand there in the old days, but nobody used a car now. The speed of business life was getting slower.

He travelled to the city deep in thought. He was thinking about his new appointment, and he looked down at his uniform.

The Royal Australian Navy was very small now. It had only seven small ships, and they burned coal instead of oil. But the aircraft carrier *Melbourne* had not been changed to coal. If she burned coal, she would not be fast enough and aircraft would not be able to land safely on her.

He began to think again about his new appointment. Perhaps an officer was sick, and someone had to take his place. Or perhaps he was going to get an appointment on land. But he would rather go to sea again.

He reached the city in about an hour. He walked out of the station and got on a streetcar. There was not much other traffic and the streetcar took him quickly to the few shops that were open. He began to look for two light wheels in good condition. After he found them, he took a streetcar back to the Navy Department.

He put the wheels down in one of the offices and spoke a word or two to a young officer that he knew. The officer left him and went into the Admiral's office. Peter looked anxiously down at his uniform and put his hat under his arm.

The young officer soon returned. 'The Admiral will see you now, sir,' he said.

Peter marched into the Admiral's office. He found the Admiral sitting at his desk.

'Good morning, Lieutenant-Commander,' he said. 'You may sit down.'

Peter sat down in the chair beside the desk.

'You haven't had work for some time?' the Admiral said.

'That's correct, sir.'

'Well, I've got an appointment for you – an appointment at sea. I can't put you in one of our own ships. You're going to an American ship – USS *Scorpion*.'

He looked up at the younger man. 'I understand that you've met Commander Towers.'

'Yes, sir.' Peter had met the captain of *Scorpion* two or three times. The captain was about thirty-five and came from New England. When the war began, he had been in his submarine. Peter had read his report. Towers was at that time between Kiska and Midway, but he headed for Manila. His engines were driven by nuclear power and he had travelled at full speed. On the fourth day the submarine was north of Iwojima. Towers had put his periscope up to have a look over the sea, but he could not see much. The air seemed to be full of dust. At the same time the detector on his periscope showed a large amount of radioactivity. He tried to report this to Pearl Harbor, but he got no reply. The submarine continued, and the radioactivity grew greater near the Philippines.

Next night he sent a message to Dutch Harbor. He wanted the message to be sent on to his Admiral, but he was told that many signals were not getting through. He got no reply.

On the next night he was unable to communicate with Dutch Harbor. He headed for Luzon. In the Balintang Channel he found a lot of dust and radioactivity. On the seventh day he was in Manila Bay and he looked at the city through the periscope. The detector showed less radioactivity, but it was still dangerous. He did not want to take the submarine up to the surface. He could see smoke above the city. He thought that there had been a nuclear explosion here, or more than one, perhaps. He could see nothing moving on the beach. He went closer, but his submarine touched bottom in the main channel. Now he was sure that a nuclear explosion had changed the shape of the bottom of the sea.

He rose from the bottom and started for the open sea. The coast was soon far away. That night he failed to communicate with any radio station or ship. He had now been under water for eight days. The men did not seem to be ill, but some were anxious about their homes. Finally he was able to communicate with an Australian radio station at Port Moresby. Conditions there seemed

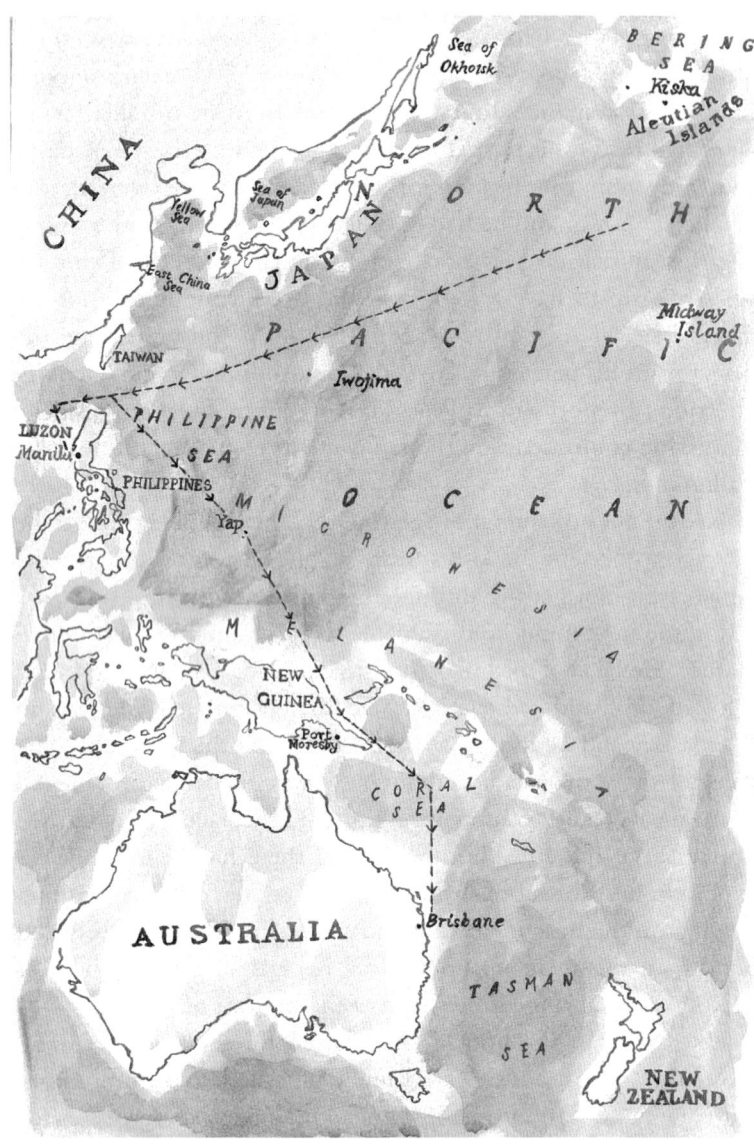

Commander Towers's journey

to be as usual. It seemed that the best course was to the south so he turned towards Yap Island and reached it three days later. There the radioactivity was low and he came to the surface.

He blew some clean air through his ship and let the men go out in groups. He was glad to find an American warship there. He crossed to the big ship in a boat. He put himself under the orders of the ship's captain, Captain Shaw.

There he learned for the first time about the Russo–Chinese war that had come out of the Russo–NATO war, which had in turn followed the Arab–Israeli war. He learned about the use of cobalt bombs by the Russians and the Chinese.

The big warship was waiting at Yap for oil. She had been there for a week and she had heard no news from the United States for the last five days. The captain had enough oil to take his ship to Brisbane, but no more.

Commander Towers stayed at Yap for six days. He hoped that no cobalt bombs would fall there. The news grew worse every day. They were unable to communicate with any radio station in the United States or Europe, but they were able to hear the news from Mexico City for two days and the news was as bad as it could be. Then they heard nothing more from Mexico City.

They could hear stations in Panama, Bogotá and Valparaiso, but these places had no news about the north. They managed to communicate with a few ships of the United States Navy. Most of them, like themselves, had a little oil. The captain of the warship at Yap ordered all US ships to go to Brisbane, and put themselves under Australian command.

Two weeks later he met them all there: eleven ships of the US Navy. Not one of them had any fuel and there was little hope of getting any. That was a year ago and they were still there.

Towers could find nuclear fuel for USS *Scorpion*, but there was none ready when the submarine arrived so they waited for some time at Williamstown. After the nuclear fuel was prepared,

Scorpion was able to move. She sailed to Rio de Janeiro, carrying nuclear fuel for another US submarine. After that *Scorpion* returned to Melbourne.

◆

All this was known to Peter Holmes, and it passed quickly through his mind. He sat in front of the Admiral's desk and thought about Commander Towers. The appointment that the Admiral offered him was a new one. There had been no Australian officer in *Scorpion* when the submarine had visited South America. He thought about Mary and his little daughter.

'How long will this appointment last, sir?' he asked.

'Perhaps a year,' replied the Admiral. 'This will probably be your last appointment, Holmes.'

'I know, sir. I'm very grateful for the opportunity. Will the ship be at sea long, sir? I'm married and we've got a baby. Things aren't easy at home, and there isn't much time now.'

The Admiral agreed. 'We're all in the same position, of course. I shall not criticize you if you don't want to accept. But if you don't accept, I can't offer much hope of anything else. The ship will be ready on the fourth of the month. That's about a week from now. Then she will sail to Cairns, Port Moresby and Port Darwin. She will report on conditions in those places. Then she will return to Williamstown. Commander Towers thinks that all this will take eleven days. After that there may be a longer trip for her. It may last two months.'

'Will there be any time between the two trips, sir?'

'I expect so. Perhaps two weeks.'

'And nothing after that?'

'We know nothing at the present time.'

The younger officer sat in thought for a moment. He thought about his wife, the baby and the milk they needed. It was summer weather, and nobody needed to cut wood for the fire. He could be home before the middle of April. That was before fires were needed in the house. Perhaps the farmer would help Mary if he was away longer. He had got the wheels for the farmer's cart. But if the electricity failed, or if the radioactivity spread south quickly . . . It was better not to think of that.

Mary would be angry if he refused the appointment. She was an officer's daughter from Southsea, England. He had met her there when he was doing his sea time with the Royal Navy.

He lifted his head. 'I should be all right for those two trips, sir,' he said. 'Is it possible to decide later about anything else? It is difficult to make plans now.'

The Admiral agreed. 'I can fix that, Holmes,' he said. 'I'll give you this job for five months, until the thirty-first of May. Report to me again when you get back from the second trip and we'll discuss the situation.'

'Very good, sir.'

'You'll report to *Scorpion* on Tuesday. That's New Year's Day. Wait outside my office for your letter to the captain. The submarine's at Williamstown with her mother ship, *Sydney*.'

'I know, sir.'

The Admiral stood up. 'Right, Lieutenant-Commander!' He held out his hand. 'I hope you'll enjoy your appointment.'

Peter Holmes shook hands. 'Thank you, sir,' he said. He paused before leaving the room. 'Do you know if Commander Towers is on board today?' he asked. 'Perhaps I could meet him and see the ship.'

'I believe he's on board,' said the Admiral. 'You can telephone to *Sydney*. An electric car is leaving from the main gate soon. Half past eleven. You'll be able to catch that.'

◆

Twenty minutes later Peter Holmes was sitting by the driver of the electric car. It took him to Williamstown. The streets were empty and the vehicle moved along at thirty kilometres an hour. At Williamstown Holmes walked down to *Sydney*, an aircraft carrier. He went on board, and down to the officers' living quarters.

There were only about twelve officers there. The captain of *Scorpion* was one of them. He came forward, smiling, to meet Peter.

'I'm glad to see that you could come down,' Towers said.

'I hoped you wouldn't mind, sir. I'm joining the ship on Tuesday. I was at the Navy Department. Perhaps I could have a look around the ship.'

'Of course,' said the captain. 'Admiral Grimwade told me that you were joining us. I was glad to hear it. I'd like you to meet some of my officers.' He turned to the others. 'This is my chief officer, Mr Farrell, and this is my engineering officer, Mr Lundgren.' He smiled. 'We need some good engineers to look after our motors. Here are Mr Benson, Mr O'Doherty and Mr Hirsch.' The captain turned back to Peter. 'Shall we have a drink before lunch, Commander?'

The Australian thanked him and the captain rang a bell.

'How many officers do you have in *Scorpion*, sir?' Peter asked.

'Eleven if you include the chief officer. She's quite a big submarine, of course, and we carry four engineering officers.'

'You must have a big living area.'

'There's a crowd when we're all there together, but that doesn't happen very often in a submarine. We've got a bed for you, Commander.'

They had lunch in *Sydney* and then they went down into *Scorpion*. She was the biggest submarine that Peter Holmes had ever seen. Her engines used nuclear power. In addition to her eleven officers, she carried about seventy other men.

Peter spent about an hour in the engine room with the engineering officer, Lieutenant-Commander Lundgren. He had never served in a ship with nuclear power, so some of the

They went down into Scorpion.

equipment was new to him. When he had seen everything, he went back to the captain's quarters and they drank some coffee together.

'I have to report to you on Tuesday,' Peter said. 'Those are my orders. What time shall I come on board, sir?'

'We're going to take stores on board on Monday. The men will come on board then too.'

'I should report to you at the same time,' said the Australian. 'Some time on Monday morning?'

The captain agreed. 'I think we'll leave at midday on Tuesday. I told the Admiral I wanted to make a short trip. I have to test everything. If you're on board on Monday morning, that'll be fine.' He looked at Peter. 'Has anyone told you the real purpose of our journey?'

The Australian was surprised. 'Haven't they told you anything about it, sir?'

The American laughed. 'Not a thing. The last person who hears the orders is the captain!'

'I learned something at the Navy Department,' Peter said. 'I was told that you were making a trip to Cairns, Port Moresby and Darwin. They said that it would take eleven days. After that there would be a longer trip – about two months.'

Commander Towers was surprised. 'That's news to me,' he said. 'Where are we going? Did he tell you?'

Peter shook his head. 'He just said it would take about two months.'

There was a short silence. Then the American smiled. 'I guess that will give me something to do,' he said.

The Australian looked at him and changed the subject. 'Aren't you going away for the weekend?' he asked.

The captain shook his head. 'I'll stay around. Perhaps I'll go to the city one day.'

It did not seem the best way of spending the weekend. The

captain was far from home, and did not know a lot of people in Australia.

Peter said suddenly, 'Would you like to come to Falmouth for a night or two, sir? We have a room. My wife would like it if you could come.'

'That's extremely nice of you,' the captain said. He drank some more coffee and thought about it. People from the north rarely mixed with Australians now. Too much stood between them. Their experiences were too different; he knew that very well, and he knew that the Australian officer knew it. But he should know more about him. If he went to the Australian's home, he would learn a lot. The change would be good for him too and it would be better than the empty aircraft carrier.

'Wouldn't it be difficult for your wife?' he asked.

Peter shook his head. 'She'd like it,' he said. 'She doesn't see a lot of new faces.'

'I certainly would like to come for one night,' said the American. 'I'll have to stay here tomorrow. But a swim on Saturday would be nice. Shall I come on Saturday on the train? I must be back here on Sunday.'

'I'll meet you at the station,' Peter said. 'Can you ride a bicycle?'

'Yes, I can.'

'I'll bring another bicycle with me to the station,' Peter said. 'We live about three kilometres from the station.'

'That's a good idea,' said Commander Towers.

His own red car was just a dream now. It was probably still in the garage of his Connecticut home, with all the other things he tried not to think about. He had to live in the new world and forget the old. So now it was bicycles at the station, not a car in the garage.

Peter left and went to catch the electric car to the Navy Department. He collected his wheels, got on a streetcar, and went to the station. He got back to Falmouth at about six o'clock, hung the wheels on the bicycle and rode heavily up the hill. He reached home about half an hour later. Mary was sitting on the grass and came to meet him.

'Oh, Peter, you're so hot!' she said. 'I see you got the wheels.'

'Yes. I'm sorry I didn't come to the beach.'

'I guessed you were busy,' she said. 'We left the beach and came home at half past five. What happened about the appointment?'

'It's a long story,' he answered. 'I'll have a bath first and tell you then.'

'Good or bad?'

'Good,' he said. 'At sea until April. Nothing after that.'

'Oh, Peter, that's wonderful! Go and have your bath and then tell me about it.'

A quarter of an hour later he was telling her. At the end he asked, 'Have you ever met Commander Towers?'

She shook her head. 'Jane Freeman met him once. She said he was rather nice. Will you like serving under him?'

'I think so. He's very clever. It's going to be strange at first in an American ship. But I like him. I've asked him to stay here.'

She looked at him in surprise. 'Oh, Peter, he won't like it. It's always too sad for the people from the north. They come into Australian homes and think of their own.'

'He'll be all right. He's older than most of them.'

'How long will he stay?'

'Only one night. He has to be back in *Scorpion* on Sunday.'

'If it's only one night, it shouldn't be too bad,' she said. 'We'll have to find him plenty to do. We must keep him busy. What does he like?'

'Swimming,' he told her. 'He wants to have a swim.'

'Does he like sailing? There's a race on Saturday.'

'I didn't ask him.'

'We could take him to the cinema.'

'It might be about America,' he said. 'Pictures of America in the old days.'

'Oh!' she cried. 'That would be terrible. Was he married?'

'I don't know. I think he was.'

She thought for a moment. 'Perhaps Moira Davidson would come.'

'If she isn't drunk,' he said. 'She drinks too much.'

'She's not like that all the time,' his wife replied. 'If she comes, she'll make him laugh.'

'It's not a bad idea,' he said. 'I could tell Moira about him. I could explain about the cinema. They don't need to go there.'

Mary telephoned Moira Davidson that evening. She told her about the American. 'Can you come and help us, dear? Keep him busy.'

Moira was not sure. 'What kind of man is he?' she asked. 'Will he start to cry and tell me all about his wife? Will he say I'm just like her? Some of them do that.'

'I've never met him,' said Mary uncertainly. 'I'll ask Peter.'

She soon came back to the telephone. 'Peter says the American will beat you. He'll get drunk and hit you until you're black and blue.'

'That's better,' said Miss Davidson. 'All right. I'll come over on Saturday morning.'

On Saturday morning Peter Holmes rode down to Falmouth. He met Moira Davidson there. She arrived in a small cart with four wheels pulled by a horse. She had straight hair and a white face and was wearing bright red trousers and a bright red shirt.

'Morning, Peter!' she said. 'Where's your friend?'

'He'll be on the next train,' he said. 'What time did you leave home?' She had driven thirty kilometres to Falmouth.

'Eight o'clock,' she said. 'Terrible!'

'Have you had breakfast?'

'Yes, thanks,' she answered. They walked to the station.

'What time did you get to bed?' Peter asked.

'About half past two.'

'How do you do it?' he said. 'I couldn't do it.'

'I can,' she said. 'I can go on as long as I must. That's not long now, is it? Why should I spend time sleeping?' She laughed rather loudly. 'It doesn't make sense.'

He did not reply because she was quite right. They waited together until the train came in. They met Commander Towers, who was not in uniform.

Peter Holmes introduced him and the American remembered the bicycle.

'I haven't ridden a bicycle in years,' he said. 'I'll fall off.'

'We've got something better for you than that,' said Peter. 'Moira has brought her cart.'

'Only one horse,' said Moira. 'But we can do about twelve kilometres an hour on a flat road.'

They reached the cart and stopped. The American stood back to admire it.

'Say!' he cried. 'That's quite a cart!'

'I've got my bicycle here,' Peter said. 'I'll ride it up the hill and meet you at the house.'

Commander Towers climbed into the cart and Moira got up beside him.

'I want a drink,' she said. 'Peter's a dear, and Mary too, but they don't drink enough.'

Towers was very surprised. He had not met a girl like this for a long time. 'I'll go along with you,' he said. 'I need a drink.'

'Then that makes two of us,' she noted. She drove the cart badly. A few cars stood in the street. They had been there for a year because there was no petrol. She stopped at a hotel and they went in.

'What can I order for you?' Towers asked.

'Something strong – a large one with a lot of ice.'

He watched her while she drank. 'You drink quite a lot, don't you?' he said.

'They tell me so. What's your name?'

'Dwight,' he told her. 'Dwight Lionel.'

'Dwight Lionel Towers,' she repeated. 'I'm Moira Davidson. You're the captain of a submarine, aren't you?'

'That's right.'

She finished her drink, and he bought her another.

'How do you spend your time?' she asked.

'Fishing, generally,' he said. He remembered a holiday long ago with his wife, but he put the thought away. One must forget the past. 'I swim too. I like going to the beach.'

'There's a sailing race this afternoon,' she said. 'We can sail Peter's boat. Do you like sailing?'

'I'll say I do,' he replied. 'But come along. The Holmeses will be waiting.'

They went to the cart and got in. The horse ran off as soon as they were in it. Towers was a little surprised. How could anyone drive so badly?

They reached the house, and Peter and Mary came out to meet them.

'I'm sorry we're late, Mary,' Moira said calmly. 'I couldn't get Commander Towers away from his drink.'

'We've had quite a ride,' the submarine commander said. He got down and was introduced to Mary. Then he looked after the horse, which was very hot.

That afternoon Mary stayed at home, and the others rode bicycles to the sailing club. They got the boat out and Moira and Towers sailed it to the starting line. Peter watched the race from the beach at the club. Towers had never sailed a boat of this kind before, but he was quick to learn. Then at one point the wind blew hard and turned the boat over. With some difficulty they turned her back over and climbed in again. They completed the course in second to last position.

After they had left the boat, the three of them had a swim. The American looked round at the blue water and the bright beach. 'This is a good place here,' he said quietly. 'It's a nice little club.'

'That's because they aren't too serious about anything,' said Peter. 'A few people are coming for drinks this evening. We can have some dinner at the hotel first; that'll help Mary. Perhaps we should dress now.'

'Never be serious about anything,' Moira said. 'When do we start drinking again?'

They dressed and rode home on their bicycles. Moira talked a lot. She was hoping to help Towers forget the past.

She went off with Peter to catch the horse. 'How am I doing?' she asked.

He laughed. 'You're doing all right,' he answered.

They went to the hotel in the cart and had some dinner. Then they drove back up the hill and left the horse in the field.

People soon began to arrive for the party, and the submarine commander enjoyed himself. When the guests left, they rode away on bicycles.

'Nice party!' said Towers. 'Really nice people.'

They sat in the garden. The fresh air was good after the hot rooms. Moira demanded a large strong drink and a lot of ice, and Towers brought it.

'You should go to bed earlier,' he said.

'Why? What's the use of anything now? I never go to bed early.'

He did not try to answer that.

'Where are you going in your submarine?' she asked.

'People are saying we're going to Port Moresby.'

'Is anyone alive there still? I thought it was a dead place.'

'I believe it is. They haven't had any radio communication from there for a long time.'

'You can't go on land if it's dead, can you?'

'No,' he said, 'but somebody has to go and look some time. We won't get out of the ship if there's a lot of radiation. I won't even come to the surface.' He paused and there was silence in the garden. 'Someone should go and see a lot of places,' he went on. 'Some radio signals are still coming from a place near Seattle. The signals don't make any sense. They're just letters. Sometimes there's nothing for two weeks, and then some more signals come. Perhaps somebody's alive up there, but he doesn't know how to send messages. Somebody should go and see.'

'Could anybody be alive up there? Is it possible?'

'I don't think so. It's just possible, of course. He could be in a closed room. All his food and water could be in there with him, stored in the room. But it isn't really possible.'

'Is it true that Cairns is dead, Dwight?'

'I think so – Cairns and Darwin. Perhaps we'll have to go and see those too. Perhaps Peter is coming with us because he knows those waters.'

'Somebody was saying that they've got radiation sickness in Townsville now. Do you think that's right?'

'I don't really know,' said Towers. 'I hadn't heard it, but it might be right. It's south of Cairns.'

'Is the sickness going to spread down here until it gets us?'

'They say so.'

'Nobody ever dropped a bomb in this part of the world,' she said angrily. 'Why must it come to us? Can't anything be done to stop it?'

He shook his head. 'Not a thing. It's the wind. You can't escape from the wind. You just can't. You have to do your best, but you can't escape.'

'I don't understand it,' she said. 'People were saying once that the wind didn't blow from the north, so we should be safe.'

'We'll never be safe,' he said quietly. 'If the wind didn't blow it down here, the radiation would come in other ways. It's in the dust. There's already more here than there used to be.'

'That doesn't seem to hurt us,' she said.

There was a silence.

'Why is it taking so long, Dwight?' she asked. 'Why doesn't the wind blow the dust here now?'

'The winds blow round the earth in the north,' he explained. 'They usually blow towards the west and the east. They do the same in the south. They go round and round; they don't often blow north to south. So it's taking a long time, but the dust is coming; it's coming.'

'I won't accept it,' she cried. 'Nobody ever dropped a cobalt bomb in the south, or any other kind of bomb. We didn't do anything. Why must we die because other countries wanted a war? They're fifteen or sixteen thousand kilometres away from us. And we have to die. It's not fair.'

'It isn't fair,' he said, 'but it's coming.'

'I don't mind dying,' she said. 'But I'm going to miss so many things. I'll never leave Australia. All my life I've wanted to go to Paris. I've wanted to see the Rue de Rivoli. But now there isn't any Paris, or London, or New York.'

He smiled at her gently. 'Paris may still be there. I don't know if Paris got a cobalt bomb or not. Perhaps the sun's shining down on it now. I like to think of it like that. But people don't live there now. That's all.'

'I don't want to see a city of dead people,' she said. 'Get me another drink, Dwight.'

'I won't. You should be in bed.'

'Then I'll get it myself.' She marched angrily into the house, and soon came out with a drink. 'I was going home in March,' she cried. 'To London. I've planned it for years. I was going to spend six months in England and in Europe. Then I was coming back through America. But I can't go now. It's not fair.'

She drank the whole drink in one. 'Perhaps it'll kill me,' she said. She could not stand up very well. She laughed. 'It's really funny!' she cried. 'Mary said that I must keep you busy and help you forget the past. I mustn't let you cry!'

She began to cry herself, and fell to the floor.

Towers did not lift her up. He waited a moment, and then he went into the house. He found Mary in the kitchen.

'Mrs Holmes,' he said, 'perhaps you should go outside and look after Miss Davidson. She has had too much to drink. I think she needs someone.'

Chapter 2 Preparing to Leave

In the morning Peter went for the milk. He took the cart.

'I've got to report for duty tomorrow,' he said to the farmer. 'I won't be able to come for the milk.'

'That'll be all right,' said Mr Paul. 'Leave everything to me. Tuesdays and Saturdays I'll take the milk to Mrs Holmes.'

Peter got back to his house at eight o'clock. He had a bath, dressed and began to help Mary with the breakfast. Commander Towers appeared at a quarter to nine, and he looked fresh and clean. Moira did not appear.

Breakfast was on the table and the three of them sat down.

'Do you want another swim?' Peter asked his guest. 'It's going to be another hot day.'

'I rather like going to church on Sunday morning,' the American said. 'Is there a church here?'

'It's just down the hill,' said Mary. 'Quite near. The service starts at eleven o'clock.'

'Perhaps I'll walk down there. Will that be all right?'

'Of course, sir,' said Peter. 'I don't think we'll come with you. I have a lot to do here.'

She began to cry herself, and fell to the floor.

The captain agreed. 'Sure! I'll be back in time for lunch. Then I'll have to go back to the ship. I'll get a train at about three o'clock.'

He walked down to the church in the warm sunlight. He was early, but he went in. The little church was like the church at Mystic, his home town. He sat down and thought about his family. He planned to go home to them in September – home from his travels – and to see them all again. The boy must be older now. He could teach him to fish. He remembered his little daughter, Helen, too. She must be nearly six now. His wife, Sharon, had the job of explaining to her that he was away at sea.

Later he walked out of the church with the others, but he knew nobody there and nobody knew him. He walked up the hill and thought about *Scorpion*.

At the house he found Mary and Moira Davidson. 'The church was full,' he said, and sat down with them.

'Mary says you're going back to Williamstown this afternoon,' said Moira. 'Can't you stay and have another swim?'

He shook his head. 'I have a lot of work on board,' he said. 'We go to sea this week.'

'Do you work all the time?' Moira said.

He laughed. 'Do you do any work?' he asked.

'Of course. I'm a very busy woman. I drink and drink. Can I come and see your submarine next week?'

'No,' he said with a laugh. 'We're going to sea. I'll show it to you another time.'

◆

He travelled back to Williamstown by train. There he went on board *Sydney*. He had two rooms on the ship and one of them was his office. Lieutenant Hirsch soon appeared with a lot of messages in his hand. One of these surprised the Commander a little. It said that a government scientist was coming on board. His name was Mr J. S. Osborne.

Towers looked up at the Lieutenant. 'Say, do you know anything about Mr Osborne?'

'He's here now, sir. He arrived this morning. I put him in the officers' quarters. The duty officer will give him his own room tonight.'

'Well, well!' said the captain. 'What does he look like?'

'He's very tall and thin, sir. About thirty.'

The Commander said, 'Ask Mr Osborne to come in.'

The scientist soon arrived. 'Well, Mr Osborne,' said Towers. 'This is a surprise. I'm glad to know you.'

'It was all decided quickly,' Osborne said. 'I only heard about it the day before yesterday.'

'Are you married?'

'No.'

'Have you ever been to sea in a submarine before?'

'No,' said the scientist.

'There isn't much room,' said Towers. He looked at the man's good clothes. 'You'll need some other clothes. Ask Lieutenant-Commander Holmes about that tomorrow morning. You'll get dirty when you go down into *Scorpion*. What are you going to do there?'

'I have orders to watch the radioactivity. I understand you're going on a trip to the north.'

'Everybody understands that except me. I'll probably be told one day. Do you expect an increase in radioactivity inside the ship?'

'I don't think so. But you'll want to know about that, won't you?'

'Of course.'

They discussed scientific matters. In the evening Osborne went down into *Scorpion*. He examined the radiation detector on the periscope. There was another detector in the ship's engine room.

A message arrived for Commander Towers on the next day. It explained about the trip.

On Tuesday Towers sailed away to begin his sea tests. All afternoon they sailed round a boat which contained some radioactive material. Osborne ran about the submarine and watched his detectors. At five o'clock the tests ended and they turned away from the boat and the radioactive material. They stayed on the surface and sailed towards the west.

In the morning they were off Cape Banks. There they went down to fifteen metres, but they sometimes came up to use the periscope and to look round. Then they left the Cape and sailed into open sea. On Thursday they were north of King Island and turned the submarine towards home. They were back at Williamstown again on Friday.

That evening Dwight telephoned Moira Davidson. 'We got back safe and well,' he said.

'Can I come and see the submarine?' she asked.

'I'll be glad to show it to you. Tomorrow's the best day.'

She was glad. 'Shall I come to Williamstown station?' she asked.

'That's the best way. I'll meet you there.'

'Good! Meet the first train after half past eleven.'

She arrived on the next day in a white dress. She looked nice, but he was a little surprised about the dress in a dirty submarine.

Towers introduced her to John Osborne, but she had met him before. 'What are you doing here, John?' she asked.

'I'm part of the ship's company,' he replied.

'Are you going to live with them in the submarine? Do they know your terrible habits?' She turned away. 'Well, it's not my business,' she added.

She made a pretty picture in the officers' quarters. She had lunch with the Americans at one end of the table. After that they gave her something better to wear. A white dress was not the best choice for a submarine.

She changed her clothes, and then they took her to *Scorpion*. She asked some questions about the submarine and she looked through the periscope, but she could not understand the engines. Then Towers gave her some tea and told her about the trip.

'We're going to Cairns, Port Moresby and Darwin,' he said. 'Then we'll come back here.'

'Will you go on land? Won't there be some radiation?'

'We'll have to find out about that. If conditions are bad, we'll stay below the surface. John Osborne will help us. He's a scientist and he understands radiation.'

'Have you ever been in a radioactive place before?'

'Oh, yes. We were in it during the war. We went from Iwojima to the Philippines. Of course, we didn't go outside the ship.'

'Has anybody been in the radioactive place since the war stopped?' she asked.

'Yes, *Swordfish* – that's our sister ship – made a trip to the north. She got back to Rio de Janeiro a month ago. I've been waiting for the captain's report. I haven't seen it yet, but the submarine went a long way. She went from Florida to Maine. She went to New York, and Halifax, and Saint John's. Then she sailed up the English Channel and into the River Thames, but she couldn't get far there. She went to look at Brest and Lisbon. But then her men were starting to fall ill, and she went back to Rio.'

'Did they find anyone alive, Dwight?'

'I don't think so.'

'Think of all those cities,' she said. 'All those fields and farms, with nobody. Nothing alive. I can't imagine it.'

'I can't either,' he said. 'I don't want to try.'

'I never saw them, of course,' she said. 'I only know those places from films and books. I don't think anybody will make another film of them now.'

He shook his head. 'It wouldn't be possible,' he said. 'Nobody can go there now. Have another cup of tea.'

'No, thanks.'

They went up to the fresh air. 'Does everybody down there in the submarine always stay calm?' she asked.

'Most of us.'

'Watch John Osborne,' she said. 'I don't believe he's a calm man.'

He was surprised. He had not thought of that. 'Well, thanks,' he said. 'I'll do that.'

They went to *Sydney* and looked at some of the aircraft.

'They'll never fly again, will they?' she said.

'I don't think so.'

'Do any aircraft fly now?'

'I haven't heard of one in the air for a long time. They've got no fuel.'

She walked quietly to her small room and changed into her white dress again. She felt better then. She hated these ships. She wanted dancing and music. She wanted to get out of these metal walls. She must get out quickly. This was no place for her.

He met her in the officers' quarters. 'You look beautiful!' he said.

'I don't feel beautiful,' she replied. 'Take me to that hotel and give me a drink. After that we'll dance.'

'Anything you say.'

He left her with John Osborne while he took off his uniform. She went up into the fresh air with Osborne. At first they lost their way in the great ship, but then they reached the sunlight and the blue sea.

'I'm glad to be out of that,' she said. 'Are you having fun?'

He thought for a moment. 'Yes, I think I am. It's going to be rather interesting.'

'Looking at dead people through a periscope. I can think of funnier sorts of fun.'

'The radioactivity may be less now,' the scientist said. 'I don't think we'll discover anything good, but we have to find out.'

'Is that fun?'

'Yes, it is. You won't face things, that's your trouble. You've got to face the facts of life.'

'All right,' she agreed angrily. 'I'll face them next September. That's the date that you scientists have given us.'

'Don't be too sure about September,' he said. 'It may come earlier or later than that.'

'Don't you know?' she asked.

Commander Towers appeared and walked towards them. 'I couldn't find you,' he said.

'Be careful, sir,' said Osborne. 'She's very angry.'

'Take me away, Dwight,' she said.

Towers took her to a hotel, and they had a few drinks. Then they went into the city. The streetcars were the only traffic in the streets. Some people were dancing in a hotel and an Italian was playing for them. A drunk fell down near them.

'It isn't as bad as before,' she told him. 'It was worse just after the war. It's Saturday today, of course. It's very quiet on an ordinary night.'

They had a meal and talked a lot. She told him about her life. She did not work now. 'People don't want office girls now,' she said. 'There's less business in the city and a lot of offices have closed.'

'Isn't there work of any kind?' he asked.

'None that I can do.'

He tried to let her enjoy the evening. He talked about things that she understood. After dinner they danced and then he paid the bill. The city was quieter now, but some men were drunk in the streets and could not walk straight.

At the station, she thanked him for a nice evening. 'When do you go north?' she asked.

'I don't know. Not yet. A message came in just before we left.

I have to report to the Navy Department on Monday. Lieutenant-Commander Holmes is coming too. Perhaps we'll leave on Monday afternoon.'

'Come and find me when you get back.'

'I will. Perhaps we could go sailing.'

He stood and watched her go. She was soon lost in the crowd. She was rather like his wife Sharon. Or perhaps he was forgetting his wife now. He turned away and went to catch his train to Williamstown.

◆

On Monday morning he went to the Navy Department. Peter Holmes went with him. They waited to see Admiral Sir David Hartman. A short time later they were invited into his office.

The Admiral got up to meet them. 'Good morning,' he said. 'The Prime Minister wants to see you before you go. We'll go to his office in a minute. But before we do that, I want to give you this. It's the report of the captain of *Swordfish* about his trip. He went from Rio de Janeiro to the North Atlantic.'

The American took the report and looked at it closely.

'He found a lot of radioactivity,' the Admiral said. 'It was greater in the north than in the south. He went down near Parniba and stayed under the water for the whole trip. He came to the surface again near Cape São Roque.'

'How long was he below the surface, sir?'

'Thirty-two days. Well, take it away and look at it. It gives news of conditions in the north. If you want to communicate with him, he's at Montevideo now.'

'Are things getting dangerous in Rio, sir?'

'Yes, a bit.'

They left the Navy Department and got into an electric car. It took them silently through the empty streets. Soon they were sitting with the Prime Minister, Mr Donald Ritchie.

He said, 'I wanted to see you, Commander Towers, to tell you something about your trip. You are going to Cairns, Port Moresby and Darwin. You will report on conditions in those places. Look for any signs of life, people or animals. And birds, if you can.'

'That's going to be difficult, sir,' Dwight said.

'Yes. I understand you're taking a scientist with you.'

'Yes, sir. Mr Osborne.'

The Prime Minister passed a hand across his face. 'Well, I don't expect you to put yourselves in danger. In fact, you must not do that. We want you back here with your ship. We want your men here in good health. Your scientist will guide you. We want all the news that you can get. If the radiation is weak, you should land. You should go into the towns. But I don't think the radiation will allow that.'

'I shall have to go below the surface south of Townsville,' said the American.

The Prime Minister said heavily, 'Yes. There are still some people alive in Townsville. You can only go there if the Navy Department decides that you can.' He lifted his head and looked at the American. 'That may seem hard to you, Commander, but you can't help them so don't give them hope by showing your ship. We know something about conditions in Townsville. We are still in communication with them.'

'I understand that, sir.'

'That brings me to the last order,' the Prime Minister said. 'You cannot take anybody on board your ship during the trip. If you want to do that, you must get the permission of the Navy Department by radio. None of you must communicate with other people. They might be radioactive. Is that quite clear?'

'Quite clear, sir.'

The Prime Minister rose to his feet. 'I hope to see you again, Commander Towers, two weeks from now.'

Chapter 3   The First Journey

Nine days later USS *Scorpion* came to the surface. First the captain put up his periscope and checked his position. Then John Osborne checked the radiation with his detectors. The *Scorpion* rose, a long grey submarine. She was moving towards the south.

Some of the officers and men came up from below, and clean air began to blow through the ship. Everyone was glad to be in the fresh air and to see the rising sun. They had all been below the surface for over a week.

The submarine stayed on the surface and moved towards the coast of Queensland. The captain reported their position by radio.

Between Cairns and Port Moresby in the Coral Sea they had met only one ship. There seemed to be nobody alive on board. All her boats were in place, but they could not go on board. There was too much radiation. So they photographed her through the periscope and left her.

'We can't say much in our report,' said Osborne.

'That's right,' the captain agreed. 'But we did see that dog.' They had in fact learned very little during the trip. They had moved towards Cairns on the surface but they had stayed inside the submarine. The radiation was high outside. They moved with great care; they even spent one night without moving at all. It might be dangerous to move in the dark.

When they sailed in towards the land, the town looked normal. The sun was shining on the beach and on the mountains behind. Through the periscope they could see streets and shops. They saw beautiful trees and houses, and a hospital. Some cars stood in the streets and one or two flags were flying. They went up the river but they saw little. There were a few boats, but no big ships. They could not see far because the top of the periscope was low in the water. It seemed like Sunday on land. A large black dog appeared and noticed the periscope.

They had stayed in the river for two hours. They called through a loud hailer, but nobody replied. The whole town was silent.

They turned the ship round and went out a little way. They could see the Strand Hotel and some of the shops again. They stayed there for a time, still calling, but they got no answer.

They moved out to sea again. The captain did not want to be near the land when night came. They had learned nothing there except some facts about the radioactivity. Cairns looked exactly as it had looked before. The sun shone in the streets, and the trees were bright on the distant hills. It was a nice place, but nobody lived there now. The only thing alive seemed to be a dog.

Port Moresby had been the same. From the sea they could see nothing wrong with the town. Through the periscope they saw a ship. She had a ladder up the side. Two more ships lay on the beach. Perhaps a storm had put them there.

The captain called through the loud hailer and they stayed there for some hours. There was no reply.

◆

Two days later they reached Port Darwin. They lay in the port below the town. They could not see much from there, only the roof of Government House and part of the Darwin Hotel. They moved around and called through the loud hailer. They examined some boats through the periscope but they could learn nothing.

'People are all in bed,' said John Osborne. 'If a man's ill, he goes to bed. Animals go into a quiet corner to die too.'

'That's enough about that,' said the captain.

'It's true,' the scientist replied.

'Right! It's true. Now we won't talk about it any more.'

They left Port Darwin as they had left Cairns and Port Moresby. They went back to the south and down the coast of Queensland, moving below the surface. They were getting tired

The only thing alive seemed to be a dog.

now. They talked little until they came up to the surface three days after they left Darwin. They all felt better after breathing some fresh air.

'Our trip is like the experience of *Swordfish*, of course,' Dwight said. 'She saw nothing in the States or in Europe.'

Peter took the report of *Swordfish* from the top of a cupboard. He had read it a number of times, and he knew it well. He turned the pages. 'It's true,' he said. 'There's nothing here about conditions on land.'

'We couldn't look anywhere on land and they couldn't either,' the captain said. 'Nobody will ever know much about radioactive places. And that's true of the whole of the northern part of the world.'

'We can't see them, and it's a good thing,' said Peter.

'I think that's right,' said the captain. 'There are some terrible things in the world now. Nobody should want to see them.'

'I was thinking about that last night,' John Osborne said. 'Have you ever thought that nobody will ever see Cairns again? Or Moresby? Or Darwin?'

'Nobody could see more than we've seen,' the captain agreed.

'Who could go there except us?' said Osborne. 'And we won't go there again.'

'That's true. I don't think they'll send us back there again. I never thought of this, but you're right. We're the last living people that will ever see those places.' Dwight paused. 'And we saw nothing.'

'There should be an account of all this,' Peter said. 'Is anybody writing a history of these times?'

'I haven't heard of one,' Osborne said. 'What's the use of writing a history that no one will ever read?'

'I'd like to read a history of this last war.' said the American. 'I was in it for a short time but I don't know a thing about it. Has anybody written anything?'

'Not a history,' said Osborne. 'We know some facts, of course, but there are a lot of things that we don't know.'

'I'd like to read about the things that we do know,' the captain said.

'What kind of things, sir?'

'Well, how many bombs were dropped? Nuclear bombs, I mean.'

'They think about 4,700,' said Osborne. 'But perhaps there were more than that.'

'How many of these were the big bombs?'

'Most of them, I think. All the bombs dropped in the Russo–Chinese War were the big kind. Most of them contained cobalt.'

'Why did they use cobalt?' Peter asked.

'I don't know,' the scientist replied. 'Probably to get more radioactivity. I can't tell you more than that.'

'I think I can tell you,' said the American. 'I learned about this kind of war at Yerba Buena, San Francisco. Some commanding officers went there a month before the war and we were told about these things. The officers there expected a war between Russia and China. They told us what might happen.'

'What did they tell you?' asked John Osborne quietly.

The captain considered for a minute. Then he said, 'It was about ports – ports with warm water. No ice in the winter. Russia hasn't got a port which doesn't freeze in the winter. There's Odessa, of course, but that's on the Black Sea. If a ship wants to leave Odessa and reach the oceans, she has to go past the Bosphorus and Gibraltar. In times of war Russian ships can't pass there. Murmansk and Vladivostok can stay open, of course. They can break the ice; they have ships for that. But those ports are a very long way from any other place. I mean a Russian place which produces anything. They said at Yerba Buena that Russia really wanted Shanghai.'

'Is that convenient for their Siberian factories?' the scientist asked.

'Yes,' the captain answered. 'During the Second World War they moved a lot of their factories to the east, as far as Lake Baikal. They built new towns and everything else. Well, it's a long, long way from those places to Odessa. Shanghai's only about half the distance.' He paused.

'There was another thing that they told us,' he went on. 'China had more people than Russia. A lot more. It had more and more factories. Russia had millions and millions of square kilometres of empty land, so she was afraid of an attack by China. She wanted fewer Chinese near her borders, and she wanted Shanghai. So the result was nuclear war.'

'But if she used cobalt,' said Peter, 'she couldn't follow and take Shanghai. Think of the radiation there.'

'That's true. But nobody could live in North China for a number of years. She could drop the bombs in the right places. Then the radioactivity would cover all China to the sea. If there was any more, it would go across the Pacific Ocean. If any of it reached the States, Russia's eyes wouldn't fill with tears. Certainly she couldn't follow the bombs and take Shanghai for a number of years. But she would get it in the end.'

Peter turned to the scientist. 'How long would it be before people could work in Shanghai?'

'After a cobalt bomb? I couldn't guess. It depends on a lot of things. More than five years, I think. Less than twenty. But you just can't say.'

Dwight agreed. 'The Russians would get there first. They would arrive before the Chinese or anyone else.'

'What did the Chinese think of all this?' John Osborne asked.

'Oh, they had a very different idea. They didn't especially want to kill Russians. They wanted to change them. They wanted Russians to grow things and do nothing else. Then they wouldn't want Shanghai or any other port. They aimed to cover Russian factories with radiation. So the Russians couldn't use the machines for ten years or more. The Chinese planned a small amount of radiation. It would not go far around the world. They didn't try to hit a city. They just wanted to drop a cobalt bomb sixteen kilometres to the west of it and let the wind do the rest.' He paused.

'When all the Russian factories were dead,' he went on, 'the Chinese could walk in at any time. They could keep away from radioactive places. Then later they could enter the towns.'

'The machines would be old and useless,' Peter said.

'Yes. But the war would be easy.'

'Do you think that actually happened?' John Osborne asked.

'I don't know,' said the American. 'Perhaps nobody knows.'

They sat in silence for a few minutes.

'Was this after the Russians bombed Washington and London?' Peter said.

'The Russians never bombed Washington,' Dwight said. 'The aircraft were Russian, but the men were Egyptians. They came from Cairo.'

'Are you sure that's true?'

'It's true enough. They shot down the one that landed at Puerto Rico. It was on its way home. They only knew that it was Egyptian after the bombing of Leningrad and Odessa and the Russian nuclear centres.'

'Do you mean that we bombed Russia by mistake?' It was a terrible thought.

'That's right, Peter,' said Osborne. 'It's an official secret, but it's true. First was the bomb on Naples. That was done by the Albanians, of course. Then there was the bomb on Tel Aviv. Nobody knows who dropped that one. Then the British and the Americans flew some aircraft over Cairo. Next day the Egyptians sent out all the aircraft they had. Six went to Washington and seven to London. One reached Washington and one reached London. After that there weren't many American or British politicians alive.'

'The aircraft were Russian,' Dwight added. 'I believe they had Russian markings too.'

'Good heavens!' cried the Australian. 'So we bombed Russia?'

'That's what happened,' said the captain heavily.

'And the war spread,' said Osborne. 'I can understand it. London and Washington were dead. Somebody had to make decisions so army officers made them. They had to be quick before more bombs arrived. Politicians in Canberra think now that the officers made the wrong decisions.'

'But if it was a mistake, why didn't they stop the war?'

'It was extremely difficult, you know,' said the captain. 'All the politicians were dead. How do you stop a war when the politicians are dead?'

'The bombs were too cheap,' said the scientist. 'They only cost about fifty thousand pounds near the end. Every little country could have some. And every little country that had some money started to drop bombs. It thought it could beat anyone else. It could drop the bombs in a surprise attack before the other country was ready. That was the real trouble.'

'Another problem was the aircraft,' the captain said. 'The Russians had been giving the Egyptians aircraft for years. The British had done the same. And they had been giving them to Israel and to Jordan. They even gave them big aircraft, which could fly a long way. That was the big mistake.'

'Well, after that,' said Peter, 'there was a war between Russia and the West. Why was China in it?'

'I don't think anybody knows exactly,' said the captain. 'Perhaps China saw that Russia was busy. So China attacked her with nuclear bombs.' He paused. 'But it's all guessing,' he went on. 'There was no news. Most of the radio stations were soon dead and silent. The higher officers were dead so younger officers had to do the thinking.'

John Osborne smiled sadly. 'Chan Sze Lin,' he said.

'Who was he?' Peter asked.

'I don't think anybody really knows. He was an officer in the Chinese Air Force. Near the end he seems to have been in command. The Prime Minister was communicating with him and trying to stop it all. And there was another man in Russia. Nobody important. But I don't think the Prime Minister ever reached the Russians. The war only stopped when all the bombs had gone and all the aircraft were useless.'

'What would I do in those conditions?' said the American. 'I just don't know. I couldn't stop fighting if I had some bombs. If Russia was hitting the States, could I just stop?'

'They didn't know either,' said the scientist. 'Too bad! But it's not the Russians' fault. The big countries didn't start this thing. The small countries are responsible for the death of the world.'

Peter Holmes smiled sadly. 'It's hard on the rest of us.'

'You've got six months more,' said John Osborne. 'Be glad about that. You've always known that you're going to die. Now you know the date, that's all. Do everything that you want to do before the end.'

'That's the trouble,' said Peter. 'I can't think of anything better than this.'

'A prisoner in *Scorpion*?'

'I can't really believe I'm going to die soon. Can you?'

'But you've seen things.'

'I haven't seen any *damage*.'

'You can't imagine anything,' said the scientist. 'All army and navy people are the same. You think it can't happen to *me*.' He paused. 'But it can and it certainly will.'

'I can't imagine the end of the world. It's too difficult.'

'It's not the end of the world,' John Osborne said. 'It's only the end of us. The world will go on just the same. But we shan't be in it. Perhaps it'll be all right without us.'

'That's probably right,' said Towers. 'Cairns seemed to be all right. There wasn't much wrong with it, or with Port Moresby either.' He paused and thought about the trees on the coast. He had seen them through the periscope. 'We're not good enough for this beautiful world,' he said.

They went up into the fresh air and the sunlight. In the morning they reached the Heads near Sydney Harbour. Then they sailed on to the south and reached the aircraft carrier at Williamstown. The Admiral was there to meet them.

◆

Dwight Towers went to meet him.

'Well, Commander,' said the Admiral, 'what kind of trip did you have?'

'We had no problems, sir. We followed our orders, but the results are not very interesting.'

'You didn't learn very much?'

'We got plenty of facts about the radiation, sir. We couldn't go up to the surface in the north.'

'Did you have any sickness?'

'No radiation sickness, sir.'

The two men went below. Dwight showed the Admiral some notes for his report. 'I'll send it to you when it's ready, sir,' he said, 'but in fact we found out very little.'

'No signs of life in any of those places?'

'Nothing at all. Of course you can't see much from a low periscope. We saw very little of Cairns and Port Moresby, and we couldn't see Darwin at all. We could only see the front of it. We didn't see anything wrong there.'

The Admiral turned over the pages of the notes. 'You stayed some time at each place?'

'About five hours. We were calling all the time through the loud hailer.'

'And you got no answer?'

'None, sir. We thought we heard something at first; but it was only the wind.'

'Birds?'

'None at all. We saw a dog at Cairns.'

The Admiral stayed twenty minutes. Then he said, 'Well, get this report ready as soon as you can. Send a copy direct to me. It's rather a pity, but you did all that anybody could have done.'

The American said, 'I was reading that report from *Swordfish*, sir. There isn't much news about things on land. They didn't see more than we did. But I would like to suggest something, sir.'

'What's that, Commander?'

'The radiation isn't very strong in most of those places, sir. The scientist tells me that a man could work in them. He can wear special clothes to keep the radiation out, and he'll be safe. We can put him on land in any of those places.'

'Won't his clothes be radioactive when he comes back?' said the Admiral. 'How can we make them safe? That's a problem, but perhaps we can solve it. I'll suggest it to the Prime Minister. Of course, he may not want anybody to go on land, but it's an idea.'

He turned towards the ladder. 'You can have ten days,' he said. 'After that I'm not sure. I'll send you a message this afternoon.'

◆

Peter Holmes rang Mary after lunch. 'We're safely back again,' he said. 'I'll come home some time tonight, dear. I have to send off a report first. I'll take it to the Navy Department on my way. Don't meet me. I'll walk up from the station.'

'I'm glad to hear from you again,' she said. 'Have you had much to eat recently?'

'No. I'll cook some eggs when I get home. There's another

thing. One of the men was ill on board. Nothing serious but anyone who comes near me may catch it. I must keep away from Jennifer.'

He went to work, and Mary telephoned Moira.

'Did they find anybody alive?' Moira asked.

'I don't know. Peter didn't say. Do you want to see Commander Towers again?'

'Oh, he isn't important to me. He's a married man.'

'He can't be married now,' said Mary.

Later in the day Peter arrived home. Mary talked to him about Towers and told him that Moira was still thinking of him.

◆

Peter had to go to the Navy Department the next day. On his way there he met John Osborne, who suggested lunch.

'Come along to my club,' Osborne said.

They met Sir Douglas Froude at the club. He was Osborne's great-uncle and had commanded the army in the old days. They sat down with him and they all had drinks.

Sir Douglas was trying to drink a lot before he died. 'It's useless to leave all that good alcohol,' he said. 'We'll soon be dead. So I take a bottle home three days a week. We're all drinking hard since we have to finish it quickly.'

Moira telephoned Peter Holmes just as he was leaving the club. 'Will you ask Commander Towers to your place?' she said.

Peter was not sure about it. 'He may give Jennifer the illness that one of the men on board caught,' he said. 'And what would Mary say then?'

'I'll tell her Jennifer caught it from you. Will you ask him?'

'All right. But he won't come.'

'He will.'

He came. Moira met him at Falmouth station, as before, and they drove together to a hotel.

'Did you find out a lot?' she asked.

'Nothing at all,' said Dwight. 'Nothing about birds. Nothing about fish. And not much about anything else.'

'Did you catch any fish?'

'You can't catch fish when you're in a submarine,' he said.

'There's nobody alive up there, is there?' she said.

He shook his head. 'I don't think so,' he said. 'I can't be sure because we didn't go on land. You could send a man if he had the right clothes. He could wear protective clothes and be safe from the radiation. But there's a problem when he comes back to the ship. His protective clothes may be radioactive themselves.'

'Will you go again?' she asked.

'Yes, I will. We've had no orders but I think they'll send us to the States.'

She was surprised. 'Can you go there?' she said.

'Yes,' he answered. 'It's a long way. If we go, we'll have to spend a long time under water. That's hard on the men. But it's possible. *Swordfish* did it, and we could do it too.'

He told her about the journey of the *Swordfish*. 'But you can't see much through a periscope,' he said. 'It's too low in the water. The captain of *Swordfish* didn't really learn much. You can see bomb damage in a port, but you can't see radiation. We called through the loud hailer, but nobody appeared so we're fairly sure that they were all dead.'

'Someone was saying that Mackay's dead now,' she said. 'Do you think it's true?'

'I think it is,' he replied. 'The dust's coming south all the time. The scientists said it would do that.'

'How long will it be before it's here?'

'September, perhaps. Perhaps a bit before that.'

She stood up. 'I want to go somewhere,' she said. 'I must do something. Shall we dance?'

'We could sail a boat,' he said.

They found a boat and joined in one of the races. Then they had a swim. While they were doing this, Peter and Mary prepared a meal.

After the meal Moira said, 'Dwight, tell me about the journey of *Swordfish*. Did you say she went to the United States?'

'That's right. She went to a lot of places near the sea. But they were all ports – Delaware Bay, Hudson River, and places like that. They also went to look at New York. That was dangerous.'

'Why?'

'Mines. Our own mines. Every big port and every river mouth was protected by mines. It was the same on the west coast too. They took a chance and went in. But they found out nothing new. The shape of the land was changed a bit. The whole place was radioactive and there was nobody alive.'

'Did they go anywhere else?'

'Yes. To New London in Connecticut. It was their home port. Most of them had lived there or near there. Like me.'

'Did you live there?' she asked.

'Yes, I did.'

'Was it like all the other places?'

'It seems so,' he replied sadly. 'They didn't say much in the report, but the radioactivity was bad. Most of the officers and men must have been near their homes. They couldn't do anything, of course. They just stayed there for a time and then went away.'

'I'm surprised they went in there,' she said.

'They went because they knew about those mines. They were able to stay away from them. I've got a home about twenty-four kilometres away. It's in a little place called West Mystic.'

She understood his thoughts. His wife and children were real to him still. He thought about them as they used to be. He did not think of them as dead.

'What's young Dwight going to be when he grows up?' she

asked. She knew that it was a dangerous question.

'Oh,' he said, 'he'll go into the Navy, like me. It's a good life for a boy. I don't know a better life. I think he wants to do that too.'

'Does he like the sea?'

'Yes, he does. We live right near the beach. He's on or in the water most of the summer. I'll get him a boat when I go home next September.'

Suddenly he turned to her. 'You think I'm weak in the head, don't you? But I can't think in any other way.'

She stood up. 'I don't think you're weak in the head,' she said.

They walked in silence to the beach.

Chapter 4 Dreams and Reality

At breakfast next morning Mary said, 'Do you want to go to church, Commander?'

'I'd like to go if it's convenient.'

'Of course it is,' she said. 'Just go when you like. We can have tea at the club this afternoon.'

He shook his head. 'Perhaps I'll have a swim. But I must get back to the ship after supper.'

He went out into the garden and Moira found him there later. He was sitting down and looking over the bay. She sat down beside him.

'Can I come to church with you?' she asked.

He looked at her in surprise. 'Certainly you can. Do you go regularly?'

'No. I should go more often.'

'Well, I'll be glad if you come with me.'

Peter Holmes was in the garden when they left the house. Mary soon came out too.

'Where's Moira?' she asked.

'She's gone to church with the captain.'

'Moira? Gone to church?'

He laughed. 'Yes,' he said.

She stood in silence for a minute. 'I hope it's going to be all right,' she said.

'Why not? He's a good man. And she's not bad when you know her. Perhaps they'll get married. Lots of things are a bit strange just now. But they'll be all right.'

She wanted to move two trees before supper. Then they could grow more useful things in their places. 'We could save some money,' she said. 'We could grow our own food.'

He went to look at the trees. 'I could pull them down,' he said. 'Then there would be some wood to burn. We could make a good fire next year. But the wood's too green now.'

They happily planned their garden for the next ten years. The morning passed quickly. They were still discussing the trees when Moira and Dwight came back. Moira heard their conversation.

'They won't be *here* in six months,' she said. 'Why are they talking like that? They won't need food next year.'

'Perhaps they don't believe it,' Dwight said. He looked over the blue sea. 'Perhaps they just like to plan a garden. Don't tell them they're crazy. Everyone's a bit crazy now. Let them enjoy themselves.'

'I don't want to ruin it for them,' Moira said. 'Nobody believes it's going to happen. Everyone thinks it will pass away. Everybody's a bit crazy on that subject.'

◆

After lunch Mary sent the men into the garden because she thought it was safer for the baby. She did not want Jennifer to catch an illness from them.

'Have you heard anything about our next journey, sir?' Peter asked.

'Not a thing. Have you?'

'I heard something about an instrument to detect radio signals. We can't do that now in *Scorpion*, can we?'

'Not if we're below the surface. Do they want us to follow the radio signals?'

'I don't know, sir. They asked if the radiation detector could be put on the front periscope. Then this other instrument could be put on the other.'

'It can go on the front periscope,' said Dwight. He paused. Then he said, 'Seattle.'

'What's that, sir?'

'Seattle. Some radio signals were coming from a place near Seattle. Are they still coming?'

Peter shook his head, surprised. 'I didn't know anything about that. Is someone sending signals?'

'I'm not sure. If anyone is, he doesn't know much about radio. Sometimes a word is clear. Most times it isn't. It's like signals sent by a child.'

'Does this go on all the time?'

'I don't think so,' said Dwight. 'It's possible that someone is alive there. But he must have power of some kind. So he must have a motor. But if he has, what kind of man is he? Is he a radio engineer who can't communicate well? I don't understand it.'

'Do you think we'll go there?'

'It's possible. They always want to know about radio stations.'

That afternoon they walked down to the beach and had a swim. Moira was with them. She asked Dwight where *Swordfish* was then.

'In Montevideo, I believe.'

'Did she move there because there was less radiation?'

'Yes.'

'There was some news on the radio this morning,' said Peter. 'The radiation is coming nearer.'

They talked about other things. Moira offered to mend Dwight's clothes and also asked him to stay with her family. She lived at Berwick.

'You could meet my father,' she said. 'He'd be glad to have another man on the farm.'

He left that evening. 'I'll expect you on Tuesday,' Moira said. 'I'll meet you at Berwick station. And bring those clothes. I'll mend them.'

◆

He arrived at Berwick on Tuesday afternoon. He got out of the train and looked round. She was there to meet him.

'You've got some nice country around here,' he cried. 'Which way is your place?'

She pointed to the north. 'Over there, about five kilometres.'

'On those hills?'

'Not at the top,' she said. 'Part way up.'

He had brought a few clothes. 'I'll mend these,' she said.

He enjoyed the drive to the farm, and especially the great trees. They were like the trees in the north.

'There are plenty of them around the farm,' she said.

The country air seemed fresh and beautiful to him. They got down and walked up the hill. He carried his coat and at one place he stopped.

'It's beautiful here,' he said.

'Is it as beautiful as places in America or England?' she asked.

'Well,' he said, 'I don't know England very well. I'm told that parts of it are very beautiful. There are beautiful places in the States too. But I don't know any place like this.'

'I'm glad,' she said. 'But I've never seen the States or England.'

They reached a gate and came to a low house. It was quite large and it was painted white. Her father came out to meet them and she introduced him.

In the evening they sat in the warm sun. Dwight again talked about the beauty of the place.

'It's not as beautiful as England,' said Mrs Davidson.

'Were you born in England?' the American asked.

'Me? No. I was born in Australia. My grandfather came to Sydney in the very early days. Then we took some land in the Riverina. Some of the family are there still. I've only been home once. We went to England and Europe in 1948. That was just after the Second World War. We thought England was quite beautiful. It's probably changed a lot now.'

She went away with Moira to make the tea. Dwight stayed with the farmer.

The farmer said, 'Moira was telling me about your journey to the north.'

The captain looked at him. 'We didn't find out much.'

'So she said.'

'You can't see much through a periscope,' Dwight said. 'There's no bomb damage, or very little. It all looks the same as before, but people don't live there now.'

'It was very radioactive, wasn't it?'

Dwight agreed. 'It's worst in the north. At Cairns, when we were there, it might be possible for a person to live for a few days. But at Port Darwin nobody could live so long.'

'When were you at Cairns?'

'About two weeks ago.'

'It'll be worse now, won't it?'

'Yes. It gets worse as time goes on. In the end it'll be the same everywhere.'

'They're still saying that it'll reach here in September.'

'Yes.'

'They were saying on the radio that it's reached Rockhampton.'

'I heard that too. And Alice Springs,' the captain agreed.

'It's useless to worry about it,' the farmer said. 'Have a drink.'

'Not now, thanks.'

'It comes to us last of all,' said the farmer.

'Yes, it seems so. Cape Town will be dead before Sydney. About the same time as Montevideo. Nothing will be left in Africa or South America. Melbourne's a big city and it's far to the south. So we'll be nearly the last people alive.' He paused for a moment in thought. 'New Zealand may last a bit longer. Or most of it. And Tasmania may do the same. Two or three weeks longer, perhaps. I don't know if there's anybody in Antarctica. If there are people there, they might live for a time.'

'But Melbourne's the last big city?' said the farmer.

'It seems so.'

They sat in silence for a short time. 'What will you do?' the farmer asked then. 'Will you move your ship?'

'I haven't decided that,' the captain answered slowly. 'Perhaps I won't have to decide it. Captain Shaw in Brisbane may do that. I don't think he'll move his ship. She can't move. Perhaps he'll send me orders. I don't know.'

'Do you want to move?'

'I don't know. It wouldn't be any better if we moved. Nearly half of my men are friendly with girls in Melbourne. Some of them are married. I might move to Hobart but I can't take the girls. And they can't get there any other way. It's not kind to the men if I take them away. Perhaps they wouldn't come if I gave the orders.' He smiled. 'It's useless to give orders which people pay no attention to.'

'Could you take your ship to sea without them?'

'Yes, for a short trip. Hobart would be a short trip. It takes six or seven hours. We could take her there with twelve men, or even less. We wouldn't go below the surface if we only had a few men. And we couldn't travel far. And we couldn't do anything if we got there. We couldn't do anything if we got to New Zealand either.'

They sat in silence for a moment. 'One thing has surprised me,' the farmer said. 'Very few people have come here from the north. They don't seem to want to escape. There have been some, of course, but not a lot.'

'That's because of the radio,' said Dwight. 'The Prime Minister has been open about everything. There isn't much point in leaving home and coming here. If they came here, they would have to live in their cars. The same thing would happen again a short time later. Then they would die.'

'I believe nobody thinks it will happen,' said the farmer. 'It may happen to other people, but not to them. But then they start to feel ill and after that they want to stay at home. It's easier. You don't get better after it starts, do you?'

'I'm not sure. You *can* get better if you escape from the radioactivity. People say so, but I don't know myself. You have to go to hospital, of course. They've got some people from the north in the Melbourne hospitals now.'

'I didn't know that,' the farmer said.

'No. They don't tell us that on the radio. What's the use? These people will only get ill again in September. Will you yourself go away from here? To Tasmania, perhaps?'

'Me?' answered the farmer. 'Leave this place? No, I won't go. When it comes, I'll die here in this chair with a drink in my hand. Or I'll die in my own bed.'

Two days of holiday followed for Dwight Towers. He was busy on the farm during the day, and he learned a lot about Australian farms. The change did him good.

'I'll have to go back to the ship this afternoon,' he said one day, and asked the times of the trains.

They gave him his clothes after lunch. They were now mended and he was very grateful. Then he was on the train.

◆

He reached the aircraft carrier at about six o'clock. He found some papers on his desk and one of them was an order from the Navy Department. It was about the west coast of the United States. He had to report at the Navy Department and he had to take Peter Holmes with him. He picked up the telephone and rang Peter.

'Can you come with me to the Navy Department?' he asked. 'I have to go there. Can you come tomorrow? I hate asking you to come back, but this is important.'

'That's all right, sir. I was only going to cut down a tree. I'll be on board tomorrow.'

He was in the aircraft carrier at half past nine. He sat down with Commander Towers in his office and read the order.

'You expected this, didn't you, sir?' Peter said.

'Yes,' the captain agreed. He turned to some papers on a table. 'This is all we know about mines,' he said. 'They say that the radio station is near Seattle. They want us to examine it. Well, we have a plan of the mines there, so we should be safe enough. We're also all right for Pearl Harbor. We have a plan of those. But they don't ask us to go there. These other places – we know nothing about the mines there.'

'I think the Admiral knows that,' said Peter.

'We know nothing about Dutch Harbor,' said the captain.

'Is there any ice up there?'

'Yes. We'll have to take care in those places.'

'How will we go?'

'On the surface north of New Zealand. Then I'll go to Pitcairn Island and then north. That will take us to California in the States. We'll come home past Hawaii and have a look at Pearl Harbor.'

'How long will we be below the surface?'

The captain turned and took a paper from the desk. 'I was trying to find out last night. I don't think we'll stay long anywhere. We'll be under the water for 19,000 kilometres. That's about 600 hours. That's twenty-five days. Add two days for visits to places. That's twenty-seven days.'

'That's a long time under water,' said Peter Holmes.

'*Swordfish* was longer under water. She went for thirty-two days. The thing is to take it easy and relax.'

Holmes pointed to the map. 'There are a lot of islands south of Hawaii. We'll have to take care when we pass those. We'll be below the surface and we'll have to find our way through them. And that comes at the end of the trip. We'll be tired.'

'I know it.' The captain looked again at the map. 'We can reach Fiji from the north.'

They worked on the orders for an hour. Then the Australian said, 'This is going to be a long journey. We'll be able to tell our grandchildren about it.'

The captain looked at him quickly and then smiled. 'You're right,' he said.

The captain telephoned the Navy Department and made an appointment for the following morning at ten o'clock. After that Peter Holmes left and took the next train to Falmouth.

He got there before lunch and rode his bicycle up the hill. He was hot when he reached home, so he had a bath and then a meal. He told Mary about the order.

'They want us to make a long journey in the Pacific,' he said. 'We'll go to Panama, San Diego, San Francisco, Seattle, Dutch Harbor and then home. We may call at Hawaii too.'

She was not certain where some of these places were. 'That's a terribly long way, isn't it?' she said.

'It is. I don't think we'll do it all. Dwight doesn't want to go to Panama. He doesn't know anything about the mines there. If we don't go there, the trip will be shorter. But it'll be a long trip.'

'How long will it take?' she asked.

'About two months. We can't take a direct course. Dwight

doesn't want to be too long under water. We'll be below the surface for twenty-seven days. That's nearly a month without fresh air.'

'When will you start?'

'I don't know. Perhaps in the middle of next month.'

They spent the afternoon in their garden. Peter started to cut down a tree. Mary brought the baby out and put her down, but she refused to stay in one place.

'We'll have to get a pushchair for Jennifer,' she said. 'That'll keep her in one place.'

He agreed. 'I'm going into town tomorrow,' he said. 'We're going to the Navy Department. I'll go to Myers after that. They may still have some pushchairs there.'

'I hope they have some. What shall we do if they haven't any?'

'We could tie her to something.'

'We couldn't, Peter!' she cried. 'You're heartless!'

◆

Peter met his captain the next morning in the Navy Department. They went to see the Admiral, who asked Dwight for his ideas about the orders.

'Mines, sir,' said Dwight. 'Some of these places are certainly protected by mines.'

'Yes, they are,' the Admiral agreed. 'We know about the mines in Pearl Harbor and near Seattle. We know nothing about the other places.'

They talked about the journey for some time. 'I should tell you about the radiation,' said the Admiral. 'Some scientists think it won't last long. They think it's growing less. There was a lot of rain and snow in the north during last winter. The radioactive dust may be going into the sea now, but there's less in the air. Jorgensen believes this very strongly, but other scientists don't agree with him. So we want a clearer idea about what's going on.'

'I understand that, sir. It's very important.'

'If Jorgensen's right,' the Admiral said, 'there will probably be less radioactivity in the north. And even less in the far north. So we want you to go a long way north: to Kodiak and to Dutch Harbor. If there isn't much radioactivity, perhaps you'll be able to leave the ship. Perhaps you'll go outside, but don't go on land. Stay out at sea. An aircraft was sent out a short time ago. Did you hear about that?'

'No, sir.'

'Well, they sent out an aircraft with plenty of fuel. It flew from Perth to the north. It reached the China Sea somewhere south of Shanghai. That's not far enough to please the scientists but it was as far as the machine could go. The level of radioactivity was still increasing, but it was increasing more slowly towards the north. Jorgensen's very pleased about it. He says that further north than that, the level will be falling.'

'We can go to Alaska,' said the captain. 'But we'll have to watch the ice.'

They talked of the trip for some time. They decided that protective clothing must be carried. Then one or two men could perhaps go outside.

When they left the office, Dwight and Peter went their separate ways. Peter went to find John Osborne in his office in Albert Street. He told the scientist all that he had learned that morning.

'I know all about Jorgensen,' said Osborne coldly. 'The old man's crazy. He just wants to believe it. That's all.'

'Don't you believe there's less radioactivity in the north?'

'There may be a bit less. But only Jorgensen believes that the difference is important.'

Peter stood up. 'I have work to do,' he said. 'I've got to buy a pushchair for my daughter.'

'Where are you going for that?'

'Myers.'

The scientist got up from his chair. 'I'll come with you. I've got something in Elizabeth Street that I want to show you.'

He refused to tell the officer any more about it. They walked together down the centre of the empty street. When they reached the shops selling cars, they went up a smaller street. Then John Osborne took a key from his pocket and opened some big doors.

The place had been a garage. Silent cars stood in rows near the walls. All were covered with dust and dirt, and all the tyres were flat. In the middle of the floor there stood a racing car. It had only one seat and it was painted red. It was a low car, a very small car. The tyres were hard. It had been cleaned with loving care.

'What's that?' cried Peter.

'It's a Ferrari. It won a race at Syracuse before the war.'

'But how did it get here?' asked Peter.

'Johnny Bowles bought it. Then the war came and he never raced in it.'

'Who owns it now?'

'I do.'

'You?'

'Yes. I've liked motor racing all my life. I've always wanted to race, but I've never had enough money. Then someone told me about this Ferrari. Bowles died in England. I went to Mrs Bowles and offered her a hundred pounds for it. She thought I was crazy, of course, but she was glad to sell it.'

Peter walked round the little car.

'I agree with her,' he said. 'You're crazy. What are you going to do with it?'

'I don't know yet. I only know one thing. It's the fastest car in the world and I own it.'

'Can I sit in it?' Peter said.

'Of course.'

He got into the little seat. 'How fast will it go?'

'I don't really know.'

In the middle of the floor there stood a racing car.

Peter sat with his fingers on the driving wheel. 'Have you taken it on the road yet?'

'Not yet.'

He got out of the seat slowly. 'What are you going to use for fuel?'

'It needs a special kind of fuel. I've got some in my mother's back garden. I was sure about that before I bought the car.'

The two men spent some time with it. They looked at the engine, which John Osborne had cleaned. He was hoping to take the car on the road in two days.

'There isn't much traffic on the roads now,' he said with a smile. 'That's one advantage!'

They left the car and locked the garage doors. They stood for a minute in the street outside.

'We should be back from the trip in June,' Peter said. 'I'm thinking about Mary and Jennifer. Do you think they'll be safe until then?'

'Do you mean safe from the radioactivity?'

'Yes.'

The scientist stood in thought. 'I'm not sure,' he said. 'I don't know any better than other people. It may come fast or slowly. It's south of Rockhampton now. If it goes on like this, it'll reach Brisbane soon. That'll be about the beginning of June. Brisbane's about 1,300 kilometres north of us. But it may be earlier or later. I can't tell you more than that.'

'If I'm not here, what'll Mary do? I don't know. I should explain to her.'

'You may not be here. It's a dangerous trip. There's not only the radiation. There are the mines. There's ice. There are all kinds of things which may stop you returning. What happens to us if the submarine hits a large piece of ice? We may be travelling at high speed when we hit it. We may be under the surface.'

'If that happens, we'll go to the bottom,' said Peter.

'Well, let's hope we don't hit any ice,' the scientist said. 'I want to get back here and race that car.'

They turned away from the garage and walked into the main street. John Osborne turned towards his office.

'Are you going my way?' he asked.

Peter shook his head. 'I've got to find a pushchair for the baby. Mary says that we've got to have it.'

They walked away separately. The scientist was not married, and he felt glad about it.

Peter went to the shops and looked for a pushchair. He found one at the second shop he tried and took it back to Falmouth. He left the pushchair at the station, found his bicycle, and rode it to the shops.

He went to a chemist's and asked the girl there for Mr Goldie, who he knew well.

The chemist came to him in a white coat and led Peter to a quiet place at the back.

'I want to have a talk with you, please,' Peter said. 'It's about this radiation. I have to go away. I'm sailing in *Scorpion*, an American submarine. We're going a long way and we'll not be back before the beginning of June. That's the earliest date.'

The chemist thought about this.

'It's not a very easy trip,' said Peter. 'We may not come back at all.'

They stood in silence for a short time.

'Are you thinking about Mrs Holmes and Jennifer?' the chemist asked.

'Yes,' Peter said. 'I must tell Mrs Holmes about everything before I go. She may not understand yet.' He paused. 'Tell me. Just what does happen to people?'

'First they feel ill,' the chemist said. 'Then they are sick. Then it gets worse. They may feel better for a short time, but the sickness starts again very soon. Then they die because they're so weak.' He paused. 'The radiation destroys parts of the body, you understand. The body stops making blood.'

'You've got something for it, haven't you?'

'Not to make it better. I'm sorry.'

'I don't mean that. But you have something to end a person's life. Am I right?'

'We can't give you that yet, Commander. We'll all be told about a week before it arrives. The radio will tell us. Then we may give it to those who ask us. We have some medicine. It's probably going to be a very difficult decision for religious people.'

'My wife must understand about it,' said Peter. 'She'll have to look after the baby. And I may not be here when it's given out. I've got to fix all this before I go.'

'I can explain it to Mrs Holmes when the time comes,' said the chemist. 'I can tell her about the medicine.'

'I would prefer to do it myself. She'll be a bit upset.'

'Of course.' The chemist stood thinking for a moment. 'Come into the back room,' he said.

There was a case in the back room. The chemist pulled back the cover. The case was full of little red boxes in two sizes.

The chemist took out one of each size. Then he opened the smaller of the two boxes. In it there were two white tablets.

He took out the two tablets and put them away. Then he put two ordinary headache tablets in their place. He closed the red box and gave it to Peter.

'This is for anybody who can take a tablet,' he said. 'You can have that and show it to Mrs Holmes. These are just headache tablets, but one real tablet kills a person almost immediately. The other is an additional tablet. When the time comes we shall be giving these out at the shop.'

'Thanks a lot,' said Peter. 'What can you do for the baby?'

The chemist took the other box. 'The baby – or a cat or a dog – that's not so easy.'

He opened the second box and took out a small needle.

'I've got a used needle,' he said. 'I'll put it in here for you. Then you can show it to Mrs Holmes. Read the instructions on the box. Do just as they tell you. Use the needle. Press it under the skin. The baby will fall asleep quite soon.'

He put a needle in the box and gave it to Peter.

'You've been very kind,' Peter said. 'I can explain it to her now. She'll be able to get the right medicine here when the time comes?'

'Yes.'

'Will there be anything to pay?'

'No,' said the chemist. 'They're free.'

Chapter 5 Testing Relationships

Mary Holmes liked the pushchair. It was quite new and it was painted green. Peter had put it on the grass, and Mary came out to see it.

She examined it closely and was very pleased. She gave him a kiss. 'It's a beautiful present,' she said. 'And it's a pretty colour.'

She brought the baby from the house and put her in the pushchair. Then they got some drinks and watched the baby.

Later in the day Peter took the pushchair into the house. He put it in one of the rooms. Then he went outside and stood with his hands in his pockets. He touched the red boxes there. How could he tell her about them?

He told her that evening. It was before they went to bed.

'I want to have a talk before I go on the trip,' he said. He did not speak very happily.

'Why?' she asked.

'It's about the radiation. People get sick, you know. I should explain about it.'

She did not want to listen. 'That's not until September,' she said.

'We'll have to talk about it,' he said. 'I'm sorry.'

'Why? I don't understand. You can tell me about it nearer the time. Tell me just before it comes. We're not really sure that it will come here. Mrs Hildred's husband was told that it wouldn't reach us. She told me about it. It's getting slower. We don't need to worry about it.'

'Who told him that? I can tell you that it is coming. It may come in September, or it may come sooner.'

'What? Do you mean we'll all get it?'

'Yes,' he said. 'We're all going to get it. We're all going to die of it. So I want to tell you a little about it.'

'Can't you tell me nearer the time? Tell me when we know the date.'

He shook his head. 'I would rather tell you now. I may not be here when it comes. It may come when I'm away. Or I may be killed by a bus. Anything may happen.'

'There aren't any buses,' she said quietly. 'You mean the submarine, don't you?'

'I'll be happier if I tell you,' he answered. 'Then I'll know that you understand. I'll be able to remember that in the submarine.'

'All right,' she said slowly. 'Tell me.'

He thought for a moment. 'We've all got to die one day,' he said. 'Perhaps dying this way isn't worse than any other. You get ill. You start to feel sick. Then you *are* sick. It seems that you go on being sick. You can't keep any food down. You may get better for a short time, but the sickness comes back. Then you get weaker and weaker and then you die.'

'How long does all this take?' she asked.

'I didn't ask about that. It may take two or three days. If you get better, it may take two or three weeks.'

'And if everybody gets it at the same time, nobody can help you? No doctors? No hospitals?'

'I don't think there will be any. You have to fight this thing alone.'

'But you'll be here, Peter?'

'I'll be here,' he said. 'But I'm telling you this to be on the safe side.'

'Who's going to look after Jennifer if I'm alone?' she asked.

'Leave Jennifer out of it for a moment,' he said. 'The main thing is this, dear. You won't get well again. Nobody will. But you don't have to die while you're being sick. You can die when you like.'

He took the smaller of the two red boxes out of his pocket and opened it. She looked at the tablet inside.

'What's that?' she whispered. 'A headache tablet?'

'This isn't really the right one,' he said. 'It isn't the real thing. Goldie gave it to me so I can show you what to do. You just take one of these white tablets with a drink. Any kind of drink. Then you just lie back, and that's the end.'

'Do you mean you die?'

'That's right. When it gets too bad, that's the way out.'

'What's that other tablet?' she asked.

'That's a second tablet. You may lose one.'

She sat in silence. Her eyes were fixed on the red box.

'When the time comes,' he said, 'they'll tell you all about it. They'll tell everybody on the radio. Then you just go to Goldie's shop and ask the girl there for it. She'll give it to you. Then you can have it in the house. Everybody who wants it can have one.'

She reached out and took the box from him. She read the instructions printed on the side.

Then she said, 'But Peter, I can't do this. Who will look after Jennifer?'

'We're all going to die,' he said. 'Every living thing – dogs, cats and babies – everybody. I'm going to die. You're going to die. Jennifer's going to die too.'

She dropped her eyes. 'That's terrible,' she cried angrily. 'I don't

She sat in silence. Her eyes were fixed on the red box.

mind dying myself. Not very much. But Jennifer! That's a terrible thing.'

He tried to make her feel better. 'It's the end of everything for all of us,' he said. 'We're going to lose years of our lives, and Jennifer's going to lose nearly all her years. But she doesn't need to feel any pain. When the time comes, you can make everything easy for her. You'll need to be brave, but you *are* brave. I'll show you what you must do.'

He took the other red box from his pocket and began to explain. She watched him angrily.

'Let me understand this clearly,' she said coldly. 'Are you telling me that I've got to kill Jennifer?'

He knew that trouble was coming, but he had to say it.

'That's right,' he said. 'If it's necessary, you'll have to do it.'

She was suddenly extremely angry. 'I think you're crazy!' she cried. 'I'll never do that, never, never! I'll take care of her until the end. You must be completely crazy. The trouble is that you don't love her. You never have loved her. And now you're trying to make me murder her.'

She stood up. Her angry face was white. 'If you say another word, I'll murder *you*!'

He had never seen her so angry before. He got to his feet.

'As you wish,' he said sadly. 'You don't have to do this if you don't want to do it.'

'You're not being honest,' she said angrily. 'You want me to murder Jennifer and then kill myself. Then you can go off with another woman.'

He had not expected that it would be so bad. 'Don't be stupid,' he said loudly. 'If I'm here, I'll be ill myself. If I'm not here, and if you've got to do everything yourself, I'll be dead. Just think of that. I'll be dead. Try to get all this into your stupid head.'

She looked at him in angry silence.

'You must think of something else,' he went on. 'Jennifer may live longer than you.' He held up the first red box. 'You can throw these away. You can go on until you fall down. You can wait until you die. But Jennifer may not be dead. She may live for days. She'll cry and be ill alone. You'll be dead on the floor beside her. There will be nobody to help her. Then, of course, she'll die. Do you want her to die like that? If you do, I don't.' He turned away. 'Just think about it and don't be stupid.'

She stood in silence. He thought that she was going to fall, but he was too angry to help her. 'This is a time,' he said, 'when you've just got to be brave.'

She turned and ran from the room. Soon he heard her crying in the bedroom. He did not go to her. He poured a drink for himself and went outside. He sat down there and looked over the sea. He was very angry with her. She lived in a world of dreams. Women could help a man a lot sometimes, if they were brave. But while they lived in their dream world, they were like a heavy stone around a man's neck.

Later he went into the house and into the bedroom. She was in bed. There was no light and he undressed in the dark. She was lying with her back to him. He turned away from her and fell asleep. At about two o'clock in the morning he woke up. He heard her crying beside him. He stretched out a hand to hold her.

She turned towards him, but she was still crying. 'Oh, Peter, I'm sorry that I've been so stupid.'

They said no more about the red boxes. Next morning he put them in the cupboard in the bathroom. In each box he left a little note. It said that these tablets were not real. It told her that she must get the real ones at the chemist's shop. He added a few words of love. She might read them when he was dead.

◆

The good summer weather lasted until March. There was no more illness in *Scorpion* and work on the submarine progressed fast. The men had nothing else to do. Peter Holmes cut down the second tree in the garden.

◆

John Osborne started his Ferrari and drove it out on the road. He was not used to it and he did not drive it well, but he did not kill anybody.

He remembered a little town called Tooradin. There was a good place there for racing. Some drivers could still get fuel, and they took their cars there to race. Osborne took his car to Tooradin several times. The car gave him something different from his work at the office. When he drove it fast, he was very excited. On the straight parts he sometimes reached 240 kilometres an hour, but then he nearly killed himself at the corners. He could not get round them easily.

He had to spend a lot of time looking for more fuel. Other owners of racing cars were doing the same.

◆

As captain of *Scorpion*, Dwight Towers attended one of Sir David Hartman's meetings. He took Peter Holmes with him. He also took the radio and electricity officer, Lieutenant Sunderstrom, who would be useful in their discussions about the radio signals from the Seattle area.

There were a lot of officers at the meeting. One of them, Sir Phillip Goodall, said, '*Scorpion* must not go into any special danger during this trip. We want to know the results and they cannot be sent by radio. It's a long way from there, and the submarine hasn't got a powerful radio. Also, she has to stay below the surface most of the time. So she must return safely. If she can't, there's no point in going. And we need *Scorpion* for other duties. We may want her to go to South America and South Africa.' He looked round at the other officers. 'I've thought for a long time about all this and I've made some changes to the journey. *Scorpion* will not go to Panama. She will not go to San Diego or San Francisco either because there are unknown mines there. Commander Towers, please tell us your thoughts about mines.'

'Seattle is open to us,' Dwight said. 'We know the mines there and we know the mines in Puget Sound. We also know about Pearl Harbor. There won't be much danger from mines near Alaska. The ice there carries them away if there are any. But the ice itself is a problem in the far north. It's a problem, but I think we can feel our way through it. I think we can go through Puget Sound.'

Then they discussed the radio signals from Seattle. Sir Phillip Goodall had a list of the messages received.

'We don't understand most of these signals,' he said. 'They don't come at any special time. There are more in the winter than in the summer. One hundred and sixty-nine messages have been received. Two of these contained English words: one word in each message. The rest didn't mean anything. I have the messages here if anybody wants them. The two words were WATERS and CONNECT.'

The radio officer made a few notes on the paper in front of him.

Sir David Hartman asked, 'How many hours of messages were received?'

'About 106 hours.'

'And in that time only two words have come through in clear language? The rest is meaningless?'

'That is correct.'

'I don't think the words mean anything,' the Admiral said. 'It's just chance. The real question is, how are these signals sent? You need electric power to send signals. There must be some electric power there still. There may even be someone controlling that power. It's hard to believe, but it is possible.'

Lieutenant Sunderstrom spoke in a low voice to the captain. Dwight said more loudly, 'Mr Sunderstrom knows the radios at Seattle.'

The Lieutenant said, 'Perhaps I don't know all of them. But I went to classes at Santa Maria Island once. It was about five years ago. They used the same wavelength.'

'Where is Santa Maria Island?' the Admiral asked.

'Near Bremerton, sir. There are several others on that coast. This one is the main Navy School in that part of the world.'

Commander Towers opened a map and pointed to the island. 'Here it is, sir,' he said. 'It's connected to this place Manchester by a bridge.'

'How far away could signals from Santa Maria Island be heard?' the Admiral asked.

The Lieutenant said, 'I'm not certain, sir. But I think they could be heard everywhere. It's a big station. It's one of the most important stations in the Pacific Ocean.'

'You yourself never received direct signals from the station?'

'No, sir. I sailed in ships which used different wavelengths.'

'If it is Santa Maria,' said Dwight, 'we can get there easily enough.' He looked at the map. He had examined it before, but wanted to be sure. 'There are twelve metres of water quite near it. If the radiation isn't too bad, we can put an officer on land. He'll wear protective clothes, of course.'

The Lieutenant said, 'I'm ready to go myself. I know my way around that place well.'

◆

After the meeting Dwight met Moira Davidson for lunch. She was carrying a small case. He looked at it when he ordered the drinks.

'Have you been to the shops?' he asked.

She was not pleased and she opened the case. It contained a notebook and pencil.

'I'm learning to be a secretary,' she said.

He was very surprised. 'You're on a course!' he cried.

'What's wrong? You said once that I ought to work in an office. Every morning I have to be in Russell Street at half past nine. Think of that! Half past nine for *me*! I have to get up before seven!'

'That's terrible,' he said with a laugh. 'Why are you doing it?'

'Oh, it gives me something to do.'

'How long have you been studying?'

'Three days. My typing's getting quite good. I'll be able to get a good job next year.'

'Are other people doing this?'

'Yes,' she answered. 'It's a big class. I was surprised.'

'Perhaps they all want jobs.'

There was a pause.

'Have you heard about John Osborne and his car?' she asked.

He laughed. 'I certainly have. He showed it to me. It's an extremely nice car.'

'He's quite crazy,' she said. 'He'll kill himself in it.'

'He's having lots of fun,' said Dwight. 'But he mustn't kill himself before we start on our trip.'

'When do you start?'

'In about a week.'

'Is it going to be very dangerous?' she asked quietly.

There was a short pause. 'No,' he said. 'Why do you think it might be dangerous?'

'I spoke to Mary Holmes on the telephone yesterday. She seemed worried. Peter had told her something.'

'About this trip?'

'Not exactly,' she replied. 'It was something else.'

The food was brought to the table.

'It's quite a long journey,' said Dwight. 'We'll be away nearly two months. We shall be below the surface for about a month. But it isn't more dangerous than any other trip in the north. It's always a bit uncertain when we go into those places because nuclear bombs have fallen there. We may run into things, particularly when we're below the surface. The bottom of the sea may look different after the bombs. Perhaps a ship has been hit by a nuclear bomb and is lying on the bottom. We have to take care, but I don't say that it's dangerous.'

'Come back safely, Dwight,' she said softly.

He laughed. 'Of course we'll come back safely. The Admiral has given us his orders. We must return safely! The Admiral doesn't want to lose his submarine!'

She sat back and laughed. 'You're a hard man,' she said.

After the meal they went to look at some religious paintings. The girl liked them but the officer did not understand them. 'I don't like any of them,' he said.

Then they went to look at some French paintings. 'These are by Renoir,' she said. They stood in front of a painting of a river. There was a street beside the river, and some shops painted white.

'That's the kind of picture I like,' said Dwight. 'I've got a lot of time for that.'

After that she had to leave because her mother was not very well, so he took her to the station in a streetcar.

'Thanks for lunch,' she said. 'I hope you liked the pictures.'

'I certainly did. I'll go there again and see some more of them.'

'Will we be able to meet again before you go?' she asked.

'I'll be busy most days,' he said. 'But we might meet one evening, perhaps.'

They agreed to meet for dinner on the following Tuesday. She waved to him and went off into the crowd. He had nothing important to do, so he walked along the streets, and looked in the shop windows. When he came to a sports shop, he went inside and bought some fishing equipment.

'This is a present for my son,' he told the shopkeeper. 'He's ten years old.'

Chapter 6   Journey to the Pacific

Twenty-five days later USS *Scorpion* was near the first port of call of their trip. She had been under the water for ten days. She had seen land at San Nicolas Island near Los Angeles, but the Commander knew nothing about the mines there and so he stayed away from the city. She had followed the coast from Santa Barbara towards the north, staying about three kilometres from land. She was below the surface all the time and had entered Monterey Bay with care. It was a port, but they saw no sign of life on land. The Commander learned very little because he had to stay under the water. There was a lot of radioactivity in these places.

They examined San Francisco from eight kilometres outside the Golden Gate. They saw that the bridge was down, but that did not tell them much. The houses round the Golden Gate Park were badly damaged. There was little chance that anybody could live in them again. There was no sign of life anywhere. The level of radioactivity was high.

They stayed there for some hours and took photographs through the periscope. Then they went back to Half Moon Bay. They moved nearer to the coast and came up to the surface, calling through the loud hailer. The houses here were not damaged much, but there was still no sign of life on land. They waited until it was dark. Then they changed direction for the north, and followed the coast again.

They went under the water, but often came to the surface so

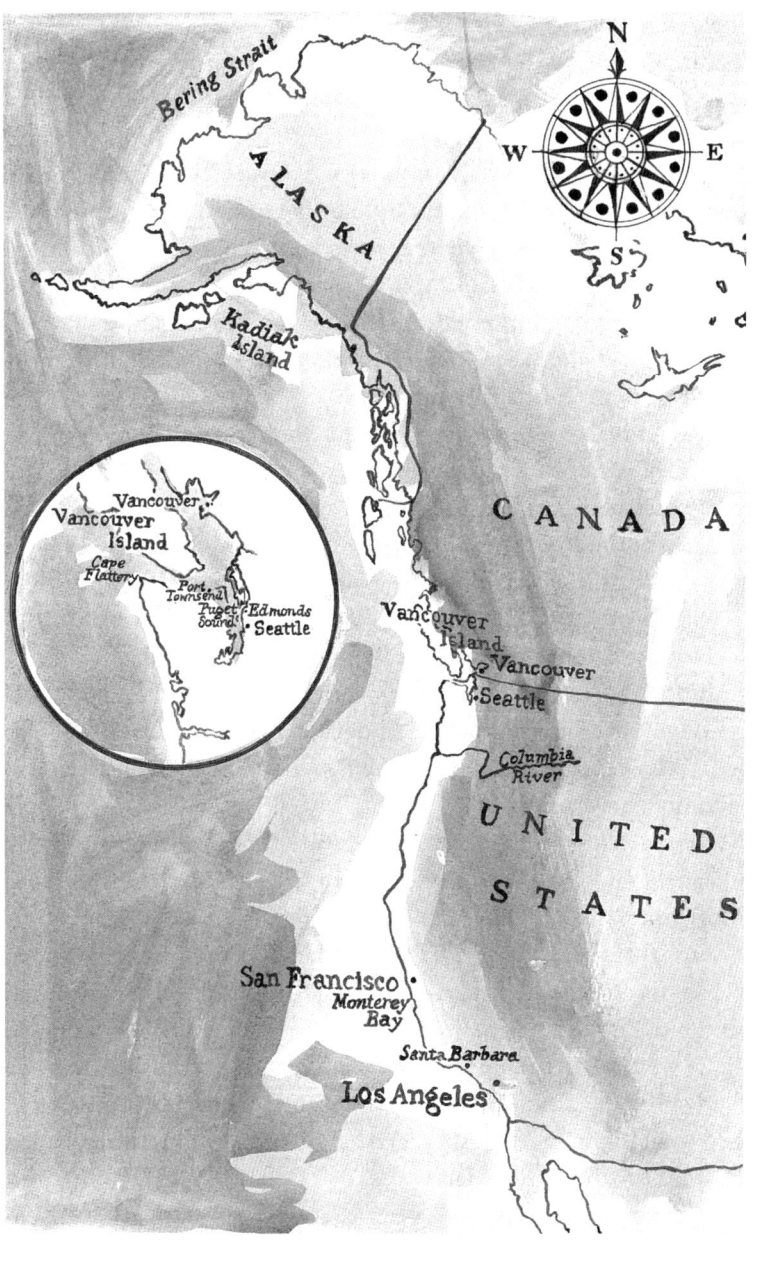

they were able to listen for the radio station at Seattle. They had heard it once. It had sent signals for forty minutes and then stopped. The messages had no meaning at all.

When they were not far from Fort Bragg, they heard it again. They came to the surface in a strong wind. The Seattle station began to send a signal, and they were able to find its position quite well. Dwight bent over the map with Lieutenant Sunderstrom. 'It's near Santa Maria,' he said. 'You were quite right.'

They stood and listened to the meaningless signals.

'It's just chance,' the Lieutenant said. 'Nobody's sending those signals. They're just happening.'

'It seems like it,' said Dwight. 'But there must be power there, and if there's power, there are people.'

'It isn't necessarily true,' the Lieutenant said.

'You're thinking of water power,' Dwight replied. 'Power from a river. But those machines can't run for two years without oil.'

'Some of them are excellent machines.'

Dwight did not answer. He turned back to the maps.

'I'll try to reach Cape Flattery in the morning,' he said. 'We'll go on as we're going now. We'll decide about our course then. If it looks safe, I'll take her in. We'll use the periscope. If we hit anything, we can come up. Perhaps we'll be able to go to Santa Maria; perhaps we won't. Are you ready to go on land if we do?'

'Sure!' said the Lieutenant. 'I'd like to get out of the ship for a short time.'

Dwight smiled. They had been below the surface now for eleven days. People's health was still good, but everybody wanted to get out of the submarine. 'Let's hope we'll get there,' he said.

'If we can't get there,' said the Lieutenant, 'perhaps I can go by land.' He pulled out a map. 'If we reached Grays Harbor, I could go to Hoquiam or Aberdeen. This road runs straight to Bremerton and Santa Maria.'

'It's 160 kilometres.'

'I could find a car, perhaps, and some fuel.'

The captain shook his head. It was not safe to go that far. There would be a lot of radioactivity from the car and from everything else. Protective clothes would not be enough.

'You've only got air for two hours,' he said. 'You'd be killed. And it isn't very important. We don't need to go there.'

They went under the water again. When they returned to the surface, the signals had stopped.

They sailed north all the next day. The health of his men was now important to the captain. He allowed them to look through the periscope. There was not much to see; but it gave them something new to do. This coast was their own home country. They could see places they knew. They could talk about their homes from long ago.

In the night they came to the surface again. They were now near the Columbia River. Lieutenant-Commander Farrell lifted the periscope and turned it round. Then he cried, 'Go and call the captain. Lights on land!'

In the next minute or two they all had a look through the periscope. They also examined the map. Dwight too bent over the map.

'On the Washington side of the river,' he said. 'The lights must be around Long Beach and Ilwaco. There's nothing in Oregon.'

From behind him Lieutenant Sunderstrom said, 'Electricity from water power.'

'I guess so. If there are lights, that explains a lot.' He turned to the scientist. 'What's the radiation outside, Mr Osborne?' he said.

'Bad, sir.'

The captain agreed. There could be no life out there. He went to the periscope himself and stood there for a long time. He did not like to take his ship nearer the coast. He could perhaps do that during the day, but it was night now.

'Right!' he said. 'We'll go on in tomorrow.'

◆

He went back to bed. Tomorrow would be a difficult day and he must get his sleep.

They came to the surface again at four o'clock in the morning. They were a little to the north of Grays Harbor. They could see no lights on land, but there were no towns and few roads here; the fact that there were no lights did not mean much. They went underwater again.

When Dwight came back at six o'clock, the day was bright. He had some breakfast and then stood near the maps. He examined the places where the mines should be.

At a quarter to eight they were near Cape Flattery. 'Right!' said the captain. 'Take her in, Commander!'

The sound of the motors dropped to a lower note. All morning they sailed between Canada and the United States. They watched through the periscope and marked their course on the map.

They could see little change on land. But in one place on Vancouver Island something had certainly happened. Near Jordan River a large part of a mountain had been burned. The burn was about eleven kilometres long and eight kilometres wide. Nothing was growing there at all.

'There's been an explosion there,' the captain said.

Soon after twelve o'clock they were near Port Townsend and they turned south towards Puget Sound. In the early afternoon they reached the little town of Edmonds. This was twenty-four kilometres north of the centre of Seattle. From the sea they could see no damage, but the level of radiation was high. No life could continue there for more than a few days.

The submarine rose to the surface and an officer took her towards the coast. They stopped a hundred metres from it and watched.

This place was the home town of Ralph Swain, and he was

invited to look through the periscope. He stood at it for a long time. Then he turned his head.

'Ken Puglia's shop's open,' he said. 'But he's left the lights on. He doesn't usually do that during the day.'

'Can you see anybody moving round, Ralph?' asked the chief sailor.

'No. But a window's broken in Mrs Sullivan's house at the top.'

He watched for three or four long minutes. Then an officer took the periscope.

The chief asked Ralph if he had seen his own house.

'No. You can't see it from the sea,' said Ralph. He seemed upset. 'The place doesn't look different,' he said. 'It all looks just the same.'

Lieutenant Benson called land through the loud hailer. He said. 'This is the US Submarine *Scorpion*. We are calling Edmonds. If anybody is listening, please come to the water's edge. Come to the end of Main Street. US Submarine calling Edmonds.'

Dwight Towers watched through the periscope. He had a good view of the place and could see the streets near the sea.

'There isn't much wrong on land,' he said. 'It's a strange thing because Boeings are made here. Why didn't the enemy destroy it?'

'It's a well-defended place,' Farrell said.

'That's true. But they were able to reach San Francisco.'

They stayed there for some time because they could see a light. They called again through the loud hailer. The captain looked at the clock.

Suddenly they all heard the noise of a metal door. The captain was surprised and looked round. Then they all heard the sounds of feet above them. Somebody was outside the ship.

Lieutenant Hirsch appeared.

'Swain got out through the escape door, sir,' he said. 'He's outside.'

Dwight was not pleased.

'Is the escape door closed now?' he asked.

'Yes, sir.'

The captain turned to the chief sailor. 'Put a man near the escape doors,' he said. 'He must guard them.'

The chief ran off and the others heard someone fall into the sea. Dwight said to Farrell, 'Try to see him. What's he doing?'

The officer pulled the periscope down as low as possible. He turned it round. The captain said to Hirsch, 'Why didn't somebody stop him?'

'I guess he was too quick. He was just sitting there. Nobody was paying him much attention. Before anybody noticed he was at the escape door. Nobody wanted to go out there after him.'

'Sure!' Dwight agreed.

From the periscope Farrell said, 'I can see him now. He's swimming towards the land.'

Dwight had a look and saw the man in the water. He spoke to Lieutenant Benson at the loud hailer.

The Lieutenant spoke into the instrument. He said, 'Swain, hear this.'

The man in the water paused and waited.

'The captain's orders are these. You will return immediately to the ship. If you return immediately, he will take you back on board. You may be radioactive, but he'll accept that danger. You will come back on board right now.'

They could all hear the reply. It was not polite.

A little smile appeared on the captain's face for a moment. He bent down to the periscope again and watched the man in the sea. The man swam to the land.

The captain spoke to Osborne. 'How long will he last?' he said.

'He'll feel nothing for a time,' the scientist said. 'He'll probably be sick tomorrow night. After that I don't know, sir. We can only guess. Everybody's different. Some last longer than others.'

'Three days? A week?'

'Not longer in this radiation.'

'And if we took him back on board?'

'If he came back, and if he were seriously ill on board, we would all die.'

Dwight put up the periscope and put his eyes to it. The man was walking up the street in his wet clothes. They saw him at the door of a shop, and he looked in. Then he turned a corner and they could not see him any more.

The captain said, 'Well, he doesn't want to come back. That's clear enough. We'll go on. Take the course for Santa Maria.'

There was silence in the submarine. Dwight Towers went slowly to his room, and Peter Holmes followed him.

Holmes said, 'Aren't you going to try to get him back, sir? I could go on land in protective clothes.'

'That's a nice offer, Commander,' said Towers, 'but I won't accept it. I thought of that myself. If we put an officer on land, he can take two men with him but he'll have to find Swain first. It might take four or five hours. If he brought him back, everybody would be in danger. We don't want radiation inside the submarine. No.'

Peter replied, 'Very good, sir. I only wanted to make the offer.'

'Sure. It was a good thing to do. We'll be coming back past this place tonight or early tomorrow. We'll stop for a short time and call him through the loud hailer.'

They went to the entrance of the Lake Washington Canal and then close to the heart of the city. It was undamaged. Some ships lay there. Most of the window glass was still in place in the high buildings. They did not go very close in. But through the periscope they could not see anything wrong at all. Many of the electric lights were still burning, but there were no people.

'It was a well-defended place, sir,' said Farrell.

There was no reason to stay there so they went out of the bay and turned towards Santa Maria Island. They could already see the great radio station. Dwight called Lieutenant Sunderstrom.

'Are you ready to go?' he asked.

'Everything's ready,' said the radio officer. 'I've only got to get into a suit.'

'Right. Your job's half done already. We know that there's still some electric power. And we're almost certain there's no life. But we're not really sure of that. You'll find the reason for those signals. You have enough air for two hours. I want you back here in an hour and a half. You won't have a watch, so I'll keep the time for you. I'll sound the siren every quarter of an hour. Once after a quarter of an hour. Twice after half an hour, and so on. When you hear the siren blow five times, you stop work. You stop everything and come back immediately. Before it sounds six times, you must be back here and clean. Is all that clear?'

'Quite clear, sir.'

'Right! I want you back on board safe. That's the main thing. I don't really want to send you at all, but I told the Admiral I would put a man on land. You will not go into any unnecessary danger. If we don't find out the whole story of the signals, it doesn't matter. But if you see signs of life, you may look more closely.'

'I understand, sir.'

'Don't bring anything back with you. Don't even bring your protective clothes into the ship.'

'Right, sir.'

The submarine moved slowly towards Santa Maria. They took the greatest care and they hit nothing below the surface. The ship stopped near the island.

Dwight found Lieutenant Sunderstrom in the protective suit. He was sitting down and waiting.

'Right!' said Dwight. 'Off you go!'

The young man stood for a moment. He tested his equipment, put one thumb in the air, and went through the escape door. He closed the door behind him.

The sunlight outside was beautiful. He was glad to be out of the ship. He unpacked a small boat and filled it with air. Then he got into the boat and left the submarine. He reached the land in ten minutes.

He began to walk on the beach and heard one sound from the submarine's siren. He turned and waved, and then walked on.

He came to a group of grey buildings. Then he crossed the road and looked into another building. A dead body lay there. It had been there a long time. It upset him a little and he left it quickly.

He went on up the road and into the main office of the Radio School. It was in a brick building. He hoped to find the cause of the radio signals in it, but every door was locked.

He went out again and looked round. He noticed another office, which was built of wood. As he walked towards it, he heard the sound of a machine. At the same moment, the siren of the submarine sounded twice.

When the sounds had died away, he heard the machine again. He did not need to search long for it. It was running well, but he did not think it would last much longer. He could hear a rough noise inside it. It needed oil.

He left the machine and went into the office building. Here all the doors were unlocked and some of them were open. The rooms on the ground floor seemed to be offices. Papers and messages lay on the floor like dead leaves. Water had caused a lot of damage here. One window had gone.

He went up to the next floor. It was the main signals room and there were two desks in it. Each of them had some grey radio equipment in front of it. All the instruments at one desk were dead and silent.

The other desk was near the window. Part of the window had been blown on to the desk. One end of it stuck out of the building and was moving gently in the wind. The 'send' key was

The wind on the moving window had been sending signals to the world.

under the other end of the moving window. He reached out and lifted the window. Then he let it fall again. It pushed the key down; and an instrument showed that a signal had been sent. The wind on the moving window had been sending signals to the world. So now one of *Scorpion*'s jobs was completed. Sunderstrom knew the cause of the strange radio signals.

He lifted the window from the desk and put it down on the floor. Then he sat down at the desk and put his hand on the key. He began to send a message in English in clear language:

'Santa Maria sending. USS *Scorpion* reporting. No life here. The station is closing down.' He repeated this message again and again. While he was doing this, the siren blew three times.

As he worked, he looked around the office. There were one or two bottles there, and he noticed some papers near a window. They were copies of the *Saturday Evening Post*.

He stopped sending messages after about twenty minutes. At the end he added a few more words: 'Lieutenant Sunderstrom sending. All in good health on board. Going north to Alaska. Closing the station down now.'

He took his hand from the key and looked at the instruments. They had done an excellent job. They had worked for two years alone and without oil or care. And they were still working! He stood up and went down to the ground floor. The siren blew four times while he was there. His work was done and he still had a quarter of an hour. He did not want to go into the other rooms. He did not want to see any more dead bodies if it was not necessary. He went upstairs again and examined the copies of the *Saturday Evening Post*. Three of them were dated after *Scorpion* had left Pearl Harbor before the war. He began to read and then the siren blew five times.

He left the office immediately and closed the door behind him. He went out of the building and walked towards the sea. He noticed another building. Some people seemed to be having a party in it. Part of a woman's dress was waving in the wind. Five men and two women were sitting at a table and there were some glasses on it.

He went closer. But then he stopped and began to feel sick. This party had been going on for more than a year. The people were dead and had been there for a very long time.

He turned away and hurried on towards the sea. He wanted now to be with other men and safe in the submarine.

When he reached the ship he took off all his protective clothes. He left the small boat and entered through a special door. Once inside he washed himself well. Then he went into the main part of the submarine.

John Osborne met him and tested his body for radiation. There was none, and he went to make his report to Dwight Towers.

'We got your signals here,' the captain said. 'They probably heard them in Australia too.'

He sent Sunderstrom to get dressed. He told the others that they would stay there that night. 'It's seven o'clock,' he said, 'and it'll soon be dark. We can't find our way through the minefields at night. We'll sail when the sun comes up.'

They watched the lights on land through the periscope. They left in the morning, but soon ran on to a sand bank. Later they managed to reach deep water and turned towards the open sea. At twenty past ten Lieutenant Hirsch called the Chief Officer to the periscope. 'A boat, sir!' he said.

The captain had a look. 'That's Swain,' he said quietly. 'He's found a boat and some petrol, and he's fishing!'

'Well, what do you think of that!' cried the Chief Officer.

'I'll talk to him,' said the captain. 'Go close to the boat.'

There was silence in the submarine while the Chief Officer gave the orders. Soon the engines were stopped, and Dwight went to the periscope.

'This is the captain speaking,' he called. 'Good morning, Ralph. How are you feeling? Any signs of sickness?'

They could all hear the reply. 'I'm doing well, Captain. I'm all right.'

'Have you got any fish yet?'

The man in the boat held a fish up. 'I'm sorry I left you like that,' he cried.

'Don't worry about that,' the captain said. 'I understand. But I'm not going to have you on board again. I'm thinking of the rest of the ship's men.'

'I know that, Captain. It's the radioactivity, isn't it? I might spread it.'

'That's right, Ralph.'

'Please ask Mr Osborne about me, sir. How long have I got?'

'He thinks you'll go for a day or two.'

From the boat Swain called, 'Well, it has been an extremely nice last day.'

Dwight laughed. 'How are things on land?' he asked.

'Everybody's dead there, Captain. I went home, but the family were dead. I went to see my girl, but she was dead too. There are no dogs or cats or birds. Nothing alive. Except for that, everything's the same as before. I'm sorry about leaving the ship, Captain, but I'm glad to be home. I've got my car and my boat and petrol for them. And the sun's shining. I'm ready to die here like this. It's better than in Australia.'

'I know,' said Dwight. 'Is there anything you want right now? We're on our way and we'll never come back.'

'Have you any tablets?' Swain asked. 'I mean those special tablets that kill you.'

'I haven't got those, Ralph. I'll put a gun out for you if you want it.'

The man in the boat shook his head. 'I've got my own gun,' he said.

The man in the boat held a fish up.

'Is there anything else you want?'

'Thanks, Captain, but I've got everything on land. Just tell the boys on board hello from me.'

'I'll do that, Ralph. And now we're going.'

◆

That evening Mary Holmes telephoned Moira. 'There's been a radio signal from them,' she said. 'They're all well.'

The girl was very surprised. 'How did they get that?' she asked.

'The signal came from that strange station. Lieutenant Sunderstrom sent it. He said they were all well.'

'That's wonderful!' Moira cried. 'Can they send a reply?'

'I don't think so. Sunderstrom was closing the station, and there wasn't anything alive there. How are you feeling, dear?'

'Better than I was five minutes ago. I'll come over to see you.'

She arrived at Falmouth station two nights later and they talked about a holiday. 'It's not nice here in the winter,' Mary said.

'Where do you want to go?' Moira asked.

'A warm place. Queensland, perhaps. We'll have to go by train, of course.'

'Queensland won't be very easy,' said Moira.

'Because of the sickness? But that's far away.'

'They've got it at Maryborough,' Moira said. 'That's only just north of Brisbane.'

'Aren't there any other warm places?'

'There are some. But the sickness is coming south day after day.'

'Do you think it'll come here?' Mary asked.

'I do.'

'So we're all going to die?'

'I expect so.'

'Will you have a drink?' Mary said.

'Not for me,' Moira replied. 'I'm a different girl now. I don't drink at home. I only drink at parties with men.'

'Are you thinking of Dwight Towers?'

'Yes,' said the girl. 'Dwight Towers.'

'Don't you ever want to get married?' Mary asked.

Moira looked into the fire. 'I wanted to get married,' she said quietly. 'I wanted to have everything you've got. But it's too late now.'

'Can't you marry Dwight?'

The girl shook her head. 'I don't think so.'

'I'm sure he likes you.'

'Yes,' she said, 'he likes me. He kissed me. But he's married already. He has a wife and two children in America.'

Mary was very surprised. 'It's not possible, my dear,' she said.

'He thinks he's going home to them,' Moira said. 'He's going to see them next September. He'll meet them in his own home town at Mystic.' She paused. 'We're all a bit crazy these days.'

'Does he really think his wife's alive?'

'I don't know. But he thinks he'll be dead next September. He thinks he's going home to his family then.'

They talked about radiation sickness and death. Then they went to look at the red boxes in the cupboard.

Eighteen days later USS *Scorpion* rose to the surface. The submarine was now near Norfolk Island. The weather was bad in the Tasman Sea in winter. The men went up into the fresh air, but it was cold outside. Their health was not good now. They had been underwater a long time and they all had white faces.

But Dwight was pleased with the trip. He had done the job, and he had brought back all the men except Swain. At one time he had been very anxious because Lieutenant Brody had been ill. But happily now the officer was a little better.

They had proved that Jorgensen was wrong. They had sailed far to the north and had reached the waters near Kodiak, Alaska. The radiation there was no less than the radiation at Seattle.

At Pearl Harbor they had learned nothing. They had sailed right into the port. None of the men had their old homes in Honolulu, and he did not put an officer on land. There was nothing important there. They saw a lot of ships in the port, and made a list of them. They also made a note of any damage, and then they left.

From the Tasman Sea they sent a signal to Australia. They reported that they would reach Williamstown soon. The reply asked about their health, and Dwight had to explain about Swain. In the middle of the morning, a more important signal arrived. The date was three days before. The signal said:

From: Commanding Officer US Naval Forces Brisbane
To: Commander Dwight L Towers USS *Scorpion*
Subject: Additional Duties
At this date you will immediately accept the duties of Commanding Officer US Naval Forces in all areas. You will decide on the positions of these forces. You will also end or continue their work with the Australian command as you decide. This makes you an admiral if you want to be one. Goodbye and good luck.
JERRY SHAW
Copy to First Naval Member Royal Australian Navy.

Dwight read this signal and then sent for Peter Holmes. He gave him the signal but did not discuss the subject.

After Peter had read it, the captain spoke. 'I guess this means that Brisbane's dead,' he said.

Brisbane was 400 kilometres north.

'They couldn't move the ships at Brisbane,' the captain said. 'They had no fuel oil.'

'Why did the Commanding Officer stay there? A man can move to the south by land.'

'He was captain of a ship, and the ship couldn't move,' Dwight said. 'A captain stays with his men.'

Towers sent a short signal in reply. He marked it to Brisbane, with a copy to the First Naval Member.

Another signal was put on his desk later. It told him that no more messages could be sent to Brisbane.

Chapter 7 A Time of Rest

Peter Holmes reported to the Admiral after their return. The ship was now at Williamstown again.

The Admiral asked him to sit down. 'I expect you want to know something about your next appointment.'

'I believe there are only two or three months more,' Peter said.

The Admiral agreed. 'That seems to be correct. You prefer to be on land at the end. You told me that before. I have not forgotten.'

'I have to think of my wife,' Peter agreed.

'Of course. *Scorpion* needs repairs. I expect you know that.'

'Yes, sir. The captain wanted to have that done.'

'Would you like to stay with her during this time? Commander Towers has asked for your appointment to continue.'

'If I stay on, sir, can I live at Falmouth? The journey takes about an hour and three quarters.'

'You must ask Commander Towers about that. I think he'll agree.'

'Thank you, sir.'

'Come back and see me again if you want to leave.' The Admiral stood up. 'Is everything all right at home?'

'Quite all right, sir.'

◆

Moira Davidson telephoned Dwight Towers on the aircraft carrier. 'I have to say well done,' she said. 'You're an admiral now, aren't you?'

'You can say well done if you like,' he replied rather sadly.

'How are you, Dwight?'

'All right. But a bit tired.' He was sleeping badly.

'Are you ill?' She thought that he seemed different.

'No, I'm not ill. But there are things that I must do. And everybody's left the ship. We've forgotten what work is after all that time at sea.'

'You should have a rest yourself,' she said. 'Can you come out to Harkaway?'

He thought for a moment. 'That's extremely nice of you,' he said. 'But I have to think of *Scorpion*.'

'Leave *Scorpion* to Peter Holmes. Come and spend a little time at Harkaway with us. It's cold and it rains a lot. Come and try it. After a few days here, you'll need a change. You'll soon be back in your submarine.'

He laughed. 'I think I can do that,' he said.

When they met, she noticed a difference in him. His face was yellow and he seemed sad. 'You're ill,' she said.

'Have a drink,' he said. 'I'm all right.'

'Have you seen a doctor?'

'We have no doctor right now.'

'You've got a fever, haven't you? And you're the Commander of all US Forces. I'll have to telephone home. You can't walk home from the station with a fever. You may die and then I'll be in trouble for killing an important naval officer.'

She went to a public telephone and spoke to her mother about Dwight's health. 'I think he's quite ill,' she said. 'He's very tired too. He'll have to go to bed when we get home. Can you light a fire in his room? And ask Dr Fletcher if he can come this evening. Dwight hasn't seen a doctor at all since he got back. He's an important person now too; tell the doctor that.'

She went back to Dwight. 'Come along,' she said. 'We have to catch a train.'

Two hours later he was in a warm bed, and the doctor arrived.

'I'm sorry, Doctor,' Dwight said. 'I'm not ill at all.'

'I understand you've been in some radioactive places,' the doctor said.

'Yes. But we never went outside into the radiation.'

'You were in the submarine all the time?'

'All the time. It isn't radiation sickness, Doctor.'

'Have you been sick?'

'Not at all.'

'You must stay in bed for a bit,' said the doctor. 'How long were you at sea?'

'Fifty-three days.'

'And how long below the surface?'

'More than half of it.'

'Are you very tired?'

The captain thought for a moment. 'Perhaps I am,' he said.

'It's nothing to worry about. But I'll come again in two days' time. Stay in bed for now. And when you get up, you should not go back to work immediately. Can you take a rest?'

'I'll have to think about it.'

The doctor left, and Moira came in. She took his empty glass from the table near the bed.

'Will you have another hot drink?' she said.

He shook his head.

'Anything to eat?'

He shook his head again and she went out.

♦

On the next day Peter Holmes had lunch with John Osborne. 'I telephoned the ship this morning,' the scientist said. 'I wanted to

She took his empty glass from the table near the bed.

speak to Dwight about the report. They told me that he's staying at Harkaway.'

Peter nodded. 'He's ill,' he said. 'Moira telephoned me last night. She told me that he wasn't coming back for a week.'

The scientist was anxious when he heard that. 'I can't wait a week,' he said. 'I'm a bit worried. Jorgensen has heard of our results. He says we haven't done our job.'

'Dwight should see the report before it goes out,' said Peter. 'Why don't you telephone Moira? Then you can take it to him at Harkaway.'

'Will she be there? Isn't she on a secretarial course in Melbourne?'

'Oh, she's at Harkaway. I don't know about the secretarial course.'

The scientist began to look happier. 'I could take it this afternoon in the Ferrari,' he said.

'How much fuel have you got? You mustn't use the car a lot. There's a good train, isn't there?'

'This is naval business,' said John Osborne. 'The report is on an important subject.' He bent towards Peter and spoke quietly. 'You remember that aircraft carrier, *Sydney*? She has a lot of fuel on board for the aircraft.'

'You mustn't touch that!' cried Peter in surprise.

'Why not? This is naval business.'

'Well, don't tell me about it. How fast does that car of yours go?'

'Over 160 kilometres an hour.'

That afternoon the scientist got the car out and Peter Holmes helped him.

'Please be careful. Don't kill anybody,' Peter said.

'They're all going to die in two months,' said the scientist.

A number of people came to push the car, and started it. It rushed away in a cloud of smoke. It had no lights and John

Osborne was a bit worried about hitting a child playing in the empty streets, but everybody could hear it. Streetcars were the only other traffic. He drove the car at 110 kilometres an hour.

He reached Harkaway in twenty-three minutes. When he got out, the farmer and his wife and daughter came out of the house.

'I've come to see Dwight Towers,' Osborne said. 'They told me he was here.'

'He's trying to get some sleep,' said Moira angrily. 'Why must you make a noise like that? That's a terrible car, John. How fast can she go?'

'Over 160 kilometres an hour. I want Dwight to see this report.'

'Oh, well, he's probably not sleeping now.'

She led the way to Dwight's bedroom. He was sitting up in bed.

'I guessed it was you,' he said. 'Have you killed anybody yet?'

'Not yet,' said the scientist. He gave the report to Dwight, who began to read it. He made a few changes to the report.

'OK, John. You can send it now.' Osborne took the report.

'Can I see the Ferrari from this window?' Dwight asked.

'Yes. It's just outside.'

The captain got out of bed and stood at the window. 'What's going to happen to it?' he asked.

'I'll drive it at the races. There isn't much time now, but the races have started early.'

'I've never raced,' said the captain. 'What do you feel when you're racing?'

'Fear. Then, when it's finished, you want to do it again.' He paused. 'If I'm killed in the Ferrari, I don't mind. It's better than the radiation sickness. I prefer to be killed in the car. And you? Will you be taking *Scorpion* out to sea again?'

'I've got no orders. I'm planning to keep her under Australian command to the end. Most of the men have girls in Melbourne.'

'You should have a rest,' the scientist said. 'You should travel a bit in Australia.'

'Is there any fishing?'

'Yes, in some of the little rivers.'

'I like fishing,' said Dwight.

Time was passing and the car had no lights, so John Osborne picked up his papers and said goodbye. On the way to the door he met Moira.

'How is he?' she said. 'What do you think?'

'Oh, he's all right. Just a bit crazy. He wants to do some fishing before we all go home.'

She watched him as he got into the small seat of the car. Then he drove noisily away.

◆

Soon after the middle of winter things felt better. At the beginning of July few people were doing any work. Broken Hill and Perth were dead. The electricity was still on. As the weeks passed, people drank less and less. Then motor-cars began to appear on the roads. Nobody cared about money any more. If you wanted food, you took it from the shops. If you couldn't find any, you went to another place. There was plenty of time because there was no work to do.

The Australian Grand Prix was early that year. It was fixed for 17th August at Tooradin, but a lot of drivers wanted to race, so some earlier races were held to choose the fastest cars.

Dwight Towers drove to one of these early races and took Moira and Peter and Mary Holmes. The field was wet with rain.

Soon one of the drivers was killed in an accident. The driver of another car also had some broken bones. A girl was killed when her car ran into the lake. There were other accidents too.

John Osborne's Ferrari was then pushed into place.

'This is the end of my life,' he thought as he got in. 'But it's better than dying from radiation sickness.'

He made a good start and went round the lake bend fast. He was behind two bigger cars, and another car, a Gipsy-Lotus, drove past him. Its driver, Sam Bailey, was going at a crazy speed. The car was not running straight; it was moving this way and that. He did not like being near it. Then some cars behind him crashed into each other and he saw one flying through the air.

Osborne was travelling behind a Jaguar. Then a Bugatti was hit by a Bentley, which was pushed into the path of the Jaguar. The Jaguar turned over twice and the driver was thrown from the car. John Osborne had no time to stop. His Ferrari hit the Bugatti at over 100 kilometres an hour.

Osborne was shaken but unhurt, but the driver of the Jaguar was dying in the long grass. The Bentley had run over him. The scientist waited for a moment, but he saw several people near the dying man so he started his Ferrari again. The wheels turned slowly but one of them made a terrible noise as it touched the body of the car. He was out of the Grand Prix! He waited for the Gipsy-Lotus to come round again, and then he got out.

He started to walk to the dying driver, and the Gipsy-Lotus went past at high speed. He did not notice any other cars, and he stopped to think. If there was only one car still in the race, he had a chance.

He started the car again and moved slowly round the field. When he reached his men, they changed the bent wheel in thirty seconds. He started again, but a damaged Bugatti was also back in the race. He soon saw that the Bugatti was moving very slowly. He managed to take second place in the race.

He stopped the Ferrari in a field, and his friends ran over to share his success. He was now allowed to race in the Grand Prix, but three of the eleven drivers in this race had been killed.

He now had to take his car to Melbourne because there was something wrong with it. It tried to turn to the left all the time.

Osborne was shaken but unhurt, but the driver of the Jaguar was dying in the long grass.

Something was broken and he needed to take it to a garage.

Sam Bailey was standing near his Gipsy-Lotus and he went to talk to him. They had a drink together and Sam showed Osborne a vehicle which had brought the Jaguar to the race.

'They won't need that now,' said Sam. 'Take it. It'll carry your Ferrari to Melbourne. But be quick. Someone else may have the same idea.'

Osborne and his men put the Ferrari on the vehicle and tied it on. Then he went to look at the Jaguar. He found the driver's wife there and he spoke to her.

'I was the driver of the Ferrari,' he said. 'I'm very sorry this has happened, Mrs Harrison.'

'You hit them at the end of the accident,' she said. 'It wasn't your fault. Don't worry. He won't have to be sick for hours like the rest of us. Say, what do you want? His car?'

'No,' he said. 'I want to carry my car away on his vehicle for repairs. I want to drive it in the Grand Prix and one of the wheels is bent.'

'You just take it, friend,' she said.

He was a bit surprised. 'Where shall I return it?' he asked.

'I won't use it. You take it.'

He thought about money. He should pay for the use of the vehicle. But the time for money had gone.

'You're very kind,' he said. 'Thanks.'

'That's all right,' she said. 'Go and win the Grand Prix.'

'How will you get back to Melbourne?'

'Oh, I'll come when they bring Don.'

Chapter 8 Last Pleasures

On the first day of August the radio said there was more sickness. It had now reached Adelaide and Sydney. It did not trouble Mary

Holmes particularly; all news was bad and a sensible person did not think about it. It was a beautiful day. That was the important thing.

Only one thing troubled her: Jennifer was getting her first tooth. She cried a lot and Mary was rather anxious. She spoke to Peter about it. 'Should we get a doctor, Peter?' she asked.

'Oh, she's all right. She isn't ill.'

Jennifer cried all night and Mary got out of bed to look after her. Peter hated all this. It often happened.

'I have to go to the Navy Department, dear,' Peter said. 'I have to be at the Third Naval Member's office at a quarter to twelve.'

'Please go to the doctor, and tell him about Jennifer. She's crying too much. There must be something wrong.'

'Don't worry him. The book says she may be ill for two days.'

'Well, she's been crying now for thirty-six hours.'

By God, she has, he thought.

'It might not be teeth,' Mary said. 'It might be something different.'

'Leave it until I get back,' he said. 'I'll be back here at four or five o'clock.'

'All right,' she said slowly.

He went out and got into his car. Saving petrol was useless now. He was glad to leave the house.

There was nobody in the Third Naval Member's office except a girl. So he went out and drove to Williamstown. He went on board the aircraft carrier.

'I want some petrol,' he said to the officer of the day. 'And I want to see Commander Towers.'

'The Commander's down in *Scorpion*, sir,' was the reply.

He walked through the cold, empty ship and down to the submarine. He met Dwight Towers as soon as he was on board.

'I came for some petrol, sir,' he said. 'Is there any work to do?'

'Plenty of petrol,' said the American, 'but nothing to do. There won't be anything to do ever again. Have you any news for me?'

Peter shook his head. 'I went to the Navy Department just now, but nobody was there, except a secretary.'

They discussed the radiation and the car race.

'Are you going back to Melbourne now?' Dwight asked.

'I was thinking of doing that – if you don't want me, sir.'

'I don't. There's nothing here. I'll ride into town with you, if I may. If you can wait ten minutes, I'll change this uniform.'

Forty minutes later they were talking to John Osborne in his garage. He was still working on the Ferrari.

'When's the Grand Prix?' Dwight asked.

'They want to have it in two weeks, but I think that's too late. I think we should race on the tenth. That's a week on Saturday. There's radiation sickness in Canberra now. It's coming close. There's even one man ill in Albury.'

'In Albury? That's only about 300 kilometres north.'

'I know. So their date for the race is too late.'

'How long have we got, John?' Peter asked.

The scientist looked serious. 'I've got it now. You've got it. We've all got it. This equipment, this door, everything has been touched by radioactive dust. The air, the water, the food – everything is getting radioactive. Some people are stronger than others, but we'll all be dead in the end. Those men want to wait nearly two weeks before they hold the Grand Prix. They're crazy. There's a meeting this afternoon, and I'm going to tell them so. How can a driver drive if he's sick?'

'You're probably right,' said Dwight. He left them in the garage. He was going to have lunch with Moira Davidson. John and Peter left too and went to have lunch together at the club.

'How's your uncle?' Peter asked.

'He has drunk quite a lot of the bottles,' said the scientist. 'Of course, he's worse than he was, but now he can go to the club in his car. That helps.'

'Where does he get his petrol?'

'From the Army, I think. He drinks a lot. He may live longer than some of us. If you get drunk, you last longer.'

They reached the club and went inside. Sir Douglas Froude was sitting in the garden room. A glass stood near him and he was talking to two old friends.

'Pull up a chair,' he said. 'We'll order some more bottles.'

John Osborne rang the bell and they sat down. 'How are you feeling now, sir?' he asked.

'Not too bad, but the doctor was right. He said that drink would soon kill me. So I'll die soon, but you'll die too. And the doctor will too. I hear you won a race.'

'I didn't win it. I was second. But I've got a place in the Grand Prix.'

'Well, don't kill yourself. But it doesn't matter much if you do kill yourself. Somebody was saying they've got the sickness in Cape Town. Do you think that's true?'

'It's true enough,' replied the younger man. 'They've had it for some days. But we still get radio signals from them.'

'So they've got it before us.'

'Yes.'

'So the whole of Africa is dead, or will be dead, before us.'

'The whole of Africa will be dead in about a week,' Osborne replied. 'A place seems to die quickly at the end, so we can't be sure of exact times. If half the people are dead, the radio may not work. So nobody knows exactly. All their food's radioactive, of course.'

'I had some good times in Africa,' said Sir Douglas. 'I was a young officer in the Army then. Does this mean that we'll be the last?'

'Not quite the last,' the younger man said. 'We'll be the last big city. They've got the sickness now in Buenos Aires and Montevideo. It's starting in Auckland. Tasmania may last two more weeks, and the South Island of New Zealand. The last people alive will be the Indians in Tierra del Fuego. But some animals will live longer.'

Sir Douglas was angry. 'What do you mean? Will they live longer than we do?'

John Osborne nodded. 'They'll all die in the end, of course. There will be nothing alive at the end of next year.'

Moira Davidson and Dwight were having lunch at a table in a corner. She noticed that he was anxious about something.

'What's troubling you, Dwight?' she asked.

'Nothing much, love. I've got another ship now. I'm in command of the whole Navy and USS *Swordfish* is at Montevideo. The radioactivity is reaching those places now. I sent a signal to the captain three days ago. In his reply he said that his ship could not come here. His men have girls there. And if they came here, they could do nothing.'

'Did you tell him that he must stay there?'

'Yes, love. I want him to take *Swordfish* out to sea. He'll sink her in deep water. Have I done right or not? I don't know. There are some secret instruments on board, of course, but there will be nobody to see them. So now the US Navy will have one ship again instead of two.'

They sat in silence for a minute. Then she said, 'Are you going to do the same thing with *Scorpion*?'

'I think so.'

Suddenly she said, 'I've had an idea, Dwight.'

'And what's that?'

'Take me up into the mountains. We could do some fishing.'

'Don't you want to watch the Grand Prix?' he said. 'John Osborne's racing in it.'

'I don't want to see dead people. We'll soon see enough of them without the Grand Prix.'

'I don't want to see the race either,' he said. 'John may die there. I'd prefer to do some fishing.' He looked across the room.

'I'm going home soon,' he said. 'I've been away a long time, but it's nearly finished now. I love my wife and she's at home. You understand that, don't you?'

'Yes,' she said. 'I understand that.' She was silent for a minute and then went on, 'You've helped me a lot in these last weeks.'

He smiled. 'We could try that fishing equipment,' he said. 'We'll go by car. How far is it?'

'We'll need petrol for 800 kilometres,' she said. 'But we don't need to worry about that. Father has a lot of petrol. We'll stay at a hotel that I know.'

She had to go to a typing test that afternoon. 'I'm not very good,' she said. 'I can't do more than fifty words a minute.' She looked at her watch. 'I must go, Dwight. I don't want to be late for the test. I'll talk to Father about that petrol. He's busy on the farm and won't need his car.'

'I could come to help on the farm,' said Dwight. 'There isn't much to do at Williamstown.'

She nodded. 'I'll tell him.'

◆

He had nothing to do at all. The ship was not going anywhere. Nearly all the men were away. No signals ever arrived now. The life of the ship was finished, though he did not like to think about that. His own life was finished too. He had nothing in the world.

He walked into the town towards Osborne's garage. He saw some cars still in the shops, but the shop windows were dirty. The streets were dirty too. The streetcars were still running, but the whole city had a bad smell. It was raining a little and the skies were grey.

He reached the garage and saw John Osborne. He was working on the car with two others. Peter Holmes was there too. He had taken off the coat of his uniform. They all seemed quite happy.

'I thought you might come,' said the scientist. 'Do you want a job?'

'Yes,' said Dwight. 'This city gives me a pain.'

'Right. Help Bill Adams to put new tyres on the wheels.'

Dwight happily took off his coat. 'You've got a lot of wheels here,' he said.

'Eleven, I think. We got some from those other cars in the race.

The American started to work, and turned to Peter Holmes. 'He made you work too,' he said.

'I'll have to go soon,' Holmes said. 'Jennifer's getting a tooth. She's been crying for two days. Imagine it! Two days.'

He left half an hour later and got into his little car. He drove away down the road to Falmouth. At home he found the house very quiet.

'How's Jennifer?' he asked.

Mary put her finger to her mouth. 'She's asleep,' she said.

He went to look at the child. 'I don't think you need a doctor,' he said.

She said that she wanted several things for the garden. One of them was a garden seat. She did not live in the real world. Everyone was going to die soon, but she wanted a garden seat.

They went into Melbourne together on the next day. She was shocked and sad at the state of the city.

'What's the matter?' she asked. 'Everything's so dirty, and there's a terrible smell.'

'The men have stopped cleaning the streets,' he said.

'But why? There's no reason.'

He did not try to explain it to her.

When they bought things, they did not need to pay for them. 'We're closing the shop tonight,' one man said. 'There are only two more weeks of life.'

Mary hated it all and wanted to go home. 'Everything smells,' she said.

'Don't you want to stay for lunch?' he asked.

She shook her head. 'I would rather go home now. We can have lunch there.'

They went home and she was happier there. There was no smell at home. Everything was clean.

'I don't want to go to Melbourne again, Peter,' she said. 'How long have we got now?'

'About two weeks. But it doesn't happen suddenly. People start to get ill, but not all on the same day. Everybody gets it in the end, though. You may get better for a short time, but it comes back. But don't be unhappy. There's nothing new about death.'

◆

Dwight Towers spent some days with the Davidsons. He did some work on the farm, but the farmer was a worried man. He was anxious about his animals. He would die before them and then what would they do?

'It really is a problem,' he said.

Dwight went back to Williamstown on Tuesday morning. He had a talk with the chief sailor. Two men were absent. Another had died in a street fight. Eleven men had returned drunk. Dwight found all this very difficult. Punishing them now was useless, but he spoke to them angrily. He told them that they must still follow orders.

On the next day one of the men returned late. He tore the man's uniform off and sent him out through the gates. After that he had no more trouble of that kind.

On Friday morning he went to the garage. John Osborne's car looked ready for the Grand Prix.

'I'm going up into the mountains,' Dwight said. 'I'm sorry that I won't see you win tomorrow. I'm going fishing.'

The scientist nodded. 'Moira told me. Catch a lot of fish.' Then he added something in a low voice. 'Tomorrow's the end of it all for me.' He looked at his car almost happily.

'I hope that's not true,' said Dwight. 'I wanted you to win.'

'The car could win, but I'm not a good driver.'

Dwight went back to his car and took the road to Harkaway. He watched the houses when he went past them. Soon they would be empty, he thought. The cats and dogs would still be alive, but all the people would be dead. After about five years the radioactivity would begin to pass away. People could live again in the houses, but there would be no people then.

He reached Harkaway in the middle of the morning. Moira was ready and they drove away before lunch. They went in Mr Davidson's Ford and Moira drove. She knew the way better than Dwight. They went through the Dandenong Mountains and had lunch near Lilydale. They reached their hotel before dark. There were a lot of cars there, and the hotel was very busy.

They met other men there who wanted to fish. The next day they managed to catch a few fish, but they quite forgot the Grand Prix. They heard the radio news later at the hotel. John Osborne had won the Grand Prix.

'I'm glad he won,' the girl said. She looked around at the calm water, the long shadows, the beautiful evening light. 'Can you believe that we shan't see all this again?'

'I'm going home,' he said quietly. 'This is a fine country, and I've liked it here. But it's not my country, and now I'm going back to my own place and my own people. I like it in Australia well enough, but I'm glad to be going home to Connecticut.'

'Will you tell Sharon about me?' she asked.

'Sure,' he said. 'She may know already.'

'What will you tell her?' She looked down at the ground.

'Lots of things,' he said quietly. 'I'll tell her that you changed a bad time into a good time for me. You knew that I could give you nothing, but you helped me. I'll tell her that you sent me back to her. I'll say that you stopped me being drunk every day. I'll tell her that you kept me for her.'

She stood up. 'We must go back to the hotel,' she said. 'But Sharon won't believe all that.'

'She'll believe it,' he said, 'because it's all true. Are you glad we came here, love?'

She nodded. 'I've been happy all day, Dwight.'

'I've been happy too,' he said. 'But we should go home tomorrow. Things will be happening down there.'

'Bad things?'

'Yes,' he answered. 'I didn't want to make the trip bad for you so I didn't say anything. But the radiation sickness has reached Melbourne. John Osborne told me before we came away. There must be more now.'

Chapter 9 The End of It All

On Tuesday morning Peter Holmes drove into Melbourne. Dwight Towers had telephoned him and they were going to meet at the office of the First Naval Member. The radio had broadcast the news about radiation sickness in Melbourne.

Mary Holmes did not want him to go.

'I've got to go,' he said. 'I'll come straight back.'

He drove to the city in deep thought. It was not days now; it was hours. He went into the Navy Department, but there were not many people there. He found Dwight Towers in uniform and alone.

The door of the Admiral's office opened and Sir David Hartman stood there. His face was serious.

'Come in, gentlemen,' he said.

In the office Towers said, 'It seems I'm in command of the US Navy now. I have to tell you that I'm taking my ship away. She will no longer be under Australian command. I can't give you the exact date, but I'm leaving soon.'

The Admiral nodded.

'Can I just go?' Dwight asked. 'Is there nothing more to do?'

'Nothing. Do you expect to return?'

'No, sir. I'm going to sink my ship outside Waratah Bay.'

'When will you go?' Peter asked quietly.

'I don't know. Seven of the men have the sickness now. Perhaps we'll go on Saturday.'

'How many are going with you?'

'Ten. I am the eleventh.'

'Are you feeling well yourself?' Peter said.

Dwight smiled. 'I thought I was. But now I just don't know. I won't want any lunch today. How are you feeling?'

'I'm all right. And Mary too – I think.'

'Go back to her now.'

'Will I see you again, sir?'

'I don't think you will,' said the captain. 'I'm going home now. I'm going to Mystic in Connecticut. I'm glad to go.'

The Admiral left the room to be sick. He looked ill when he came back. He thanked Dwight Towers for their work together. 'We have always enjoyed working with the Americans,' he said. 'Particularly on the sea. But this is the end of it.'

He held out his hand.

◆

John Osborne's old mother was dying. He had brought a doctor for her, but the doctor had not returned after the first visit. She was mainly sad about her little dog.

'I should go to the office, Mother,' Osborne said. 'Will you be all right? I'll be back before lunch.'

'I'll be quite all right now, dear,' she said. She held out her arms. 'Give me a kiss before you go.'

He kissed the old face and she lay back in the bed, smiling.

There was nobody at his office, but a report was lying on his desk. It was the usual report about radiation sickness. Half the people in Melbourne were now sick. Seven others were reported sick in Hobart, Tasmania. There were also three in Christchurch, New Zealand. The report was shorter than usual.

He walked through the empty offices. This part of his life was coming to an end. He did not stay very long. The thought of his sick mother upset him. He went out and caught one of the few streetcars that was still running. Nobody paid now for travelling on a streetcar.

In Malvern he got off the streetcar and tried to find some milk. His mother's dog needed some, but he did not find any.

He went home and found his mother dead in bed. On the table by her side there was a note. It was written in pencil. There was also a glass of water, and one of the little red boxes.

He read the note. It said:

My dear son,

I must not make the last days of your life worse. I have finished my own life and I do not want to live any longer. Just close the door and leave me in my own room. I shall be quite all right. I am so very glad that you won your race.

My very dearest love,
MOTHER.

A few tears ran down his face, but only a few. Mother had always been right, and now she was right again.

He put the dog in the garden and went to the chemist's shop. There was a girl there and she gave him one of the red boxes.

'Everybody wants these,' she said, smiling.

He smiled back at her and left the shop. He went home and gave the dog a good dinner. Then he packed his clothes in a case and took out the needle.

The dog was lying on the floor, half asleep. He pushed the needle under the dog's skin. The dog was soon dead, and John Osborne carried it to his mother's room. He put it down next to the bed and went out. He shut the door and left the house.

◆

Tuesday was a bad day for Peter and Mary Holmes. At about seven o'clock the baby was sick. It was raining and cold outside. They were ill themselves.

'Is this it, Peter?' Mary said.

'I think so. Everybody seems to be getting it.'

◆

She was feeling terrible and now she wanted to be sick. She went quietly to the bathroom. Peter was making tea in the kitchen.

He was hot and then suddenly cold again. He had to go outside, and he was sick near the garage. He felt a bit better when he came back into the house. He made some tea and took it to the bedroom.

'Come and have some tea, dear,' he called.

She noticed his wet clothes. 'Oh!' she said. 'Have you been outside, Peter?'

'I've just been sick,' he said. He could not hide it any longer.

'Oh, Peter! So have I. It must be that meat we had for supper.'

He shook his head.

'Do you think this is it?' she asked. 'Is this the end?'

'I think so,' he said. 'It's hard to be sure, of course.'

She left him and went to the window. She looked out at the garden she loved. Then she went to the kitchen. 'I'll make some breakfast,' she said. 'Perhaps we can eat some.'

He heard her singing in the kitchen, and he was very surprised. When he went there, he saw tears on her face. He took her in his arms.

He took her in his arms.

'I'm glad that we're going together,' she said. 'I didn't want to leave you. And I didn't want you to leave Jennifer and me. But together it isn't so bad. Aren't we lucky?'

◆

John Osborne went to have a last look at his Ferrari. He got into the small seat and put his hands on the wheel. He felt very ill. He knew that he could never drive again.

He was very comfortable in the little car. Why must he live any longer? This was the right place. He wanted to die here. He took out his little red box and put the two tablets into his mouth.

◆

Although Mary Holmes felt very ill, she had to look after Jennifer. The baby seemed worse. Peter himself felt a bit better, but he did not tell his wife. He knew that he was soon going to die like everybody else. He made a hot drink for Mary.

They looked at the little baby. 'I believe she's dying, Peter,' Mary said. She touched the little face.

He put his arm round her shoulder. 'So am I,' he said quietly, 'and so are you. Nobody has got very long now.'

They had their hot drinks together. 'Why did all this happen to us?' she asked. 'Was it because Russia and China started fighting?'

He nodded. 'That's the reason,' he said, 'but other countries did things too. It all started with Albania.'

'Could anything have stopped it?'

'I don't know. You just can't stop some crazy things. If one country drops a cobalt bomb on another, what happens? What can we do about it? Newspapers could help. They could stop telling lies. But they aren't sensible enough.'

She suddenly rushed away to the bathroom and was sick. He looked down at his baby. She was terribly ill. He was not feeling so ill himself, but he must not show it.

He knew that he could not live on after Mary. He could do nothing without her. He could not go anywhere. He wanted to stay with his family.

Mary called him from the bathroom, and he brought her back to the fire. She was shaking badly.

'There's no hope at all, is there?' she said.

He shook his head.

'I think I want to end it tonight,' she said. 'It'll be worse tomorrow. I'll go tonight and take Jennifer with me. Is that too terrible for you? You'll be alone.'

He kissed her. 'I think you're very sensible,' he said. 'I'll come too.'

She touched his hand. 'What must we do, Peter?'

'Get into bed and keep warm. I'll bring Jennifer into the bedroom. Then I'll shut the house and bring you a hot drink. Then we'll die in bed with the tablet. It's just like a headache tablet.'

'Remember to turn off the electricity,' she said. 'We don't want to burn the house down.'

'I'll do that,' he said.

She looked at him with tears in her eyes. 'Will you do that thing to Jennifer? That terrible thing, Peter?'

He touched her hair gently. 'Don't worry,' he said. 'I'll do that.'

◆

That evening Dwight Towers telephoned Moira Davidson. 'How are things with you, love?' he said.

'Bad,' she said. 'We're all just about finished. How are you?'

'I want to say goodbye, love. I'm taking *Scorpion* out tomorrow to sink her.'

'You won't come back?'

'No, I won't come back. We've just got this last job, and then we've finished.' He paused. 'I called to thank you for the last six months. You've helped me a lot.'

'And you've helped me, Dwight. Can I come to watch you go?'

'Sure,' he said. 'But we can't wait. The men are weak now and they'll be weaker tomorrow. We're leaving at eight o'clock.'

'I'll be there,' she said.

He gave her some messages for her father and mother. She went to find them. They were in bed and she told them about the submarine.

'I'll be back before dinner,' she said.

'He has been a good friend to you,' her mother said. 'Go and say goodbye. Then come back here. But if we're not here, you'll understand.'

She kissed them both and went to bed herself. In the morning she had a hot bath. Then she looked into her parents' room. Her mother smiled at her, but her father seemed to be asleep.

She went out to the car and drove away towards Melbourne. The city was empty. She soon reached the aircraft carrier. Nobody stopped her and she walked into the ship. She saw a man who was going down to the submarine.

'Please ask Commander Towers if he can come up,' she said.

'Sure, lady,' he replied. 'I'll ask him right now.'

Dwight soon appeared. He was looking very ill, she thought.

'How are things at home, Moira?' he asked gently.

'Bad.' She paused for a moment. 'May I come with you in the submarine, Dwight?'

'I'm sorry,' he said. 'This is a US submarine. I can't take you. It's not allowed. We must all die in our own way. I'm sorry.'

'That's all right,' she said.

He took her in his arms and kissed her. 'What time are you leaving?' she said.

'Very soon. In about five minutes. Two hours and ten minutes after that, we'll sink her.'

'I'll think of you then,' she said.

'Thanks for everything,' he said. Then he turned away and went down to the submarine.

She watched while Dwight took the submarine out. It began to rain a little. Then all the men went down inside. Dwight stayed, and waved to her. She waved back and then the submarine sailed out of sight.

She turned away from the port and looked at her watch. It was three minutes past eight. At ten minutes past ten Dwight planned to be on his way home. He was going to the home that he loved so well. There was nothing now for her at her own home. Only animals and sad memories. Dwight was going down twenty kilometres from here. Only twenty kilometres.

She hurried away through the grey and silent aircraft carrier.

She started the car and drove it at 110 kilometres an hour. She drove towards Geelong and suddenly had to stop near Corio. She felt very ill, but after a time she was able to go on.

She left Geelong and took the road to Barwon Heads. She had been along this road when she was a child. She turned right at the bridge. It was twenty minutes to ten. The sea lay before her, grey and rough. She got out of the car and then she saw the submarine.

She knew that Dwight was there. He could not see her, but she waved to him. Then she got back into the car because the wind was cold. She was feeling very ill now.

She watched the low grey shape until she could see it no more. This was the end of it – the very end. It was one minute past ten.

She took the red box out of her bag and held the tablets in her hand. She suddenly felt worse.

At ten minutes past ten she said, 'Dwight, if you're on your way already, wait for me.'

Then she put the tablets into her mouth.

ACTIVITIES

Chapter 1

Before you read
1 Discuss these questions.
    a What do you know about the effects of radiation on food, animals and people?
    b Have you seen a film or a television programme about a nuclear war? What happened in it?
2 Look at the Word List at the back of the book and discuss these questions.
    a What are the words in your language?
    b Which word describes a vehicle that travels:
        1) through the air?
        2) under the sea?
        3) over the land?

While you read
3 Circle the correct words in these sentences.
    a When the story starts, it is *summer/winter/spring* in Australia.
    b The farmer would like *Peter's cart/more money for the milk/some wheels.*
    c Peter goes to the station by *car/cart/bicycle.*
    d Peter's new job is on *an aircraft carrier/a warship/a submarine.*
    e The captain of *Scorpion* is *English/Australian/American.*
    f After the war, eleven US warships went to *Yap Island/Brisbane/Pearl Harbor.*
    g Peter takes a job for *eleven days/two months/five months.*
    h On Saturday afternoon, Commander Towers goes *sailing/horse riding/shopping.*
    i *Mary/Moira/Towers* is angry and sad because they are all going to die.

After you read
4 Answer these questions.
   a Why have Peter and Mary Holmes not used their car for a year?
   b How do people in Australia travel now?
   c Why can't the American ships leave Brisbane?
   d Why can *Scorpion* travel around the world, but other ships can't?
   e Why is Mary anxious about Commander Towers' visit?
   f How is the end of their world affecting these people?
      Commander Towers   Moira Davidson   Peter and Mary

Chapter 2

Before you read
5 Discuss these questions.
   a *Scorpion* is going to make two trips to the north. What do you think it will find?
   b What equipment does it have? What dangers will it face?

While you read
6 Are these sentences right (✓) or wrong (✗)?
   a Towers and Moira go to church on Sunday morning. .....
   b Dwight Towers will go back to his family in September. .....
   c Towers goes back to the aircraft carrier in Williamstown on Sunday afternoon. .....
   d Mr Osborne is an Australian scientist. .....
   e Osborne is going to watch the levels of radioactivity during the trips to the north. .....
   f Moira has met Osborne before. .....
   g The first trip will be to visit towns in the north of Australia. .....
   h *Swordfish* is a warship. .....
   i When *Scorpion* reaches Townsville, it must stay under the water. .....

After you read

7 Who is speaking? Who to? What do their words tell you about these people and the story?
   a 'Of course. I'm a very busy woman. I drink and drink.'
   b 'You won't face things, that's your trouble. You've got to face the facts of life.'
   c 'It isn't as bad as before. It was worse just after the war. It's Saturday today, of course. It's very quiet on an ordinary night.'
   d 'None of you must communicate with other people. They might be radioactive. Is that quite clear?'

Chapter 3

Before you read

8 Discuss these questions.
   a Why is John Osborne going on this trip?
   b What experience does he have of submarines?
   c Why is it important that they come back safely?

While you read

9 In which order do these events happen? Number the sentences 1–9.
   a *Scorpion* arrives back in Williamstown. .....
   b In Cairns they see a dog, but no people. .....
   c Holmes learns that Russia was bombed by mistake. .....
   d Peter Holmes meets Osborne's great-uncle. .....
   e Towers tell Moira about his family. .....
   f *Scorpion* meets a ship on the sea, but all the people on it are dead. .....
   g *Scorpion* goes to Port Darwin, but they see nobody in the town. .....
   h Towers and Moira go sailing. .....
   i Holmes, Towers and Osborne talk about the causes of the war. .....

After you read

10 Read these lines from the story and answer the questions.

   a 'Oh, he isn't important to me. He's a married man.'

      'He can't be married now.'

      1) Who are the speakers?

      2) Who are they talking about?

      3) Is he married, or not?

      4) Do you believe the first speaker?

   b 'What's young Dwight going to be when he grows up?' she asked. She knew that it was a dangerous question.

      'Oh,' he said, 'he'll go into the Navy, like me.'

      1) Who are the speakers?

      2) Who are they talking about?

      3) Why is her question dangerous?

Chapters 4–5

Before you read

11 Do you think there is any hope for the characters in the story? Are they all going to die? How could the book have a happier ending? Discuss your opinions.

While you read

12 Complete the sentences with these names.

Dwight   John   Mary   Sunderstrom   Peter   Goldie
Jennifer   Moira

   a .... goes to church with Dwight.

   b Mary wants .... to cut down some trees.

   c Moira takes .... to stay with her family.

   d .... owns a Ferrari.

   e Peter buys a pushchair for ....

   f Mr .... is a chemist and he tells Peter about the special tablets.

   g .... is angry and upset when she hears about the tablets.

h Mr .... has been to Seattle and knows about its radio stations.

i .... is learning to type.

After you read

13 Discuss these questions.

   a What is the main destination for *Scorpion*'s trip? Why are they going there? What dangers will they face on the journey?

   b Moira Davidson's behaviour has changed a lot since the beginning of the story. What changes has she made? Why, do you think?

   c Why are a lot of people are making plans and having dreams about their future? Who has dreams about:

     1) working as a secretary?

     2) driving a fast car?

     3) going fishing?

     4) growing food?

14 Work in pairs and have this conversation.

   Student A: You are Mr Goldie, the chemist. Tell Peter Holmes about the tablets and the needles. Answer his questions.

   Student B: You are Peter Holmes. You are worried about your family. What will happen if you do not come back from the submarine trip? Talk to the chemist.

Chapter 6

Before you read

15 Discuss these questions.

   a This chapter is called 'Journey to the Pacific'. Why is *Scorpion* making this journey?

   b Look at the map on page 75. From which direction is *Scorpion* travelling to reach Los Angeles?

   c What do you think is the answer to the mystery of the radio signals from Seattle?

While you read

16 Choose the right endings to the sentences.
    a They don't take *Scorpion* near Los Angeles, … …..
    b They stay under the water all the time, … …..
    c Ralph Swain swims to Edmonds, … …..
    d Mr Sunderstrom can go on to Santa Maria Island, … …..
    e Ralph Swain enjoys his last days, … …..
    f Mary and Moira are happy, … …..
    g Moira doesn't think that she can marry Dwight, … …..
    h *Scorpion* sails north to Alaska, … …..
    i Towers becomes the commanding officer of the US navy, … …..

1) because Sunderstrom sends a signal from Santa Maria Island.
2) because he is at home.
3) because the radiation is very high.
4) because he lived there and knows it well.
5) because the radiation reaches Brisbane.
6) because he is wearing a protective suit.
7) because they hope the radiation is lower in the far north.
8) because he loves his family in the US.
9) because the captain knows nothing about the mines there.

After you read

17 Discuss these questions.
    a How were the radio signals sent from Seattle? How did they have power?
    b Why didn't the US navy officers leave Brisbane and come to Melbourne?

18 Work in pairs and have this conversation.
    Student A: You are Ralph Swain. You are fishing in your little boat near Edmonds. Talk to Commander Towers.
    Student B: You are Dwight Towers. Ask Swain what he found on the land in Edmonds. Ask him how he feels, and if he wants a gun.

Chapters 7–8

Before you read

19 Discuss these questions.
  a No one has anything more to do now. They can only wait for the end. What do you think these people will do for the last two months?
  Peter and Mary   Dwight and Moira   John Osborne
  b If you were fit and well but had only two months to live, what would you do?

While you read

20 These names all appear in these chapters. Use them to complete the sentences.
Melbourne   *Sydney*   Montevideo   Falmouth   Tooradin   Ferrari
Cape Town   the Dandenong Mountains   *Scorpion*   Harkaway
  a Peter will spend the next two months repairing ....
  b He will live in .... and travel to work.
  c Towers is ill and goes to .... to rest.
  d Osborne takes Peter's report to Towers in his ....
  e He gets petrol for the journey from the ....
  f The Australian Grand Prix car race will be held at ....
  g Osborne has to take the car to .... for repairs.
  h The last city in Africa to get the sickness is ....
  i The submarine *Swordfish* is staying in ....
  j A lot of people go to .... for the fishing.

After you read

21 Discuss these questions.
  a Most people have now stopped working. What effect does this have on people's lives?
  b Suddenly there is a lot of petrol for everyone to use. Why?

22 Work in pairs and have this conversation.

Student A: You are a radio reporter. You are interviewing John Osborne after the Grand Prix race. Congratulate him on winning the race, and ask him about the early race, when he and a lot of other drivers crashed. Ask him about his car, his life and his work.

Student B: You are John Osborne. You have just won the Grand Prix in your Ferrari. Talk to the reporter and answer his questions.

Chapter 9

Before you read

23 Chapter 9 is called 'The End of It All'. There is no happy ending to this story. How do you think the end will come for these characters?

Peter Holmes   Mary Holmes   Jennifer Holmes   Dwight Towers
Moira Davidson   John Osborne

While you read

24 In which order do these events happen? Number the sentences 1–8.

  a Dwight thanks Moira for her company over the last six months. .....
  b John Osborne goes back to his Ferrari for the last time. .....
  c The sickness comes to Melbourne. .....
  d Peter and Mary both start to feel ill. .....
  e Moira takes the tablets. .....
  f Dwight sails out to sea in *Scorpion*. .....
  g John Osborne's mother dies. .....
  h Moira goes to visit *Scorpion*. .....

After you read

25 Look back at Activity 23. What does happen to these people? How does each of them spend their last days?

Writing

26 Write Peter Holmes's report on *Scorpion*'s visit to Santa Maria Island.

27 Which character in the story do you feel closest to? Explain why.

28 Write a short account of the events in the story from the point of view of either Moira Davidson or Mary Holmes.

29 Dwight says, 'Everyone's a bit crazy now.' Describe how three of the characters in the story behave in a way which is 'a bit crazy'.

30 Write one of the notes that Peter Holmes left for his wife and daughter in the red boxes before he sailed to the Pacific.

31 Imagine that you are Dwight Towers. Before you take *Scorpion* out for the last time, you write a letter to your wife, Sharon, in Mystic. Tell her about your last months in Australia and your friendship with Moira Davidson.

32 Describe the relationship between Peter and Mary Holmes. Is this your idea of a good marriage?

33 Imagine that you are Ralph Swain. Write a diary of your last three days in Edmonds. Start when you leave the *Scorpion*.

34 Write a happier ending to the story. The radiation does not reach the south of Australia. Choose one of the characters and describe what happens to him or her.

35 Explain how the story made you feel and if you enjoyed reading it.

Answers for the Activities in this book are available from the Pearson English Readers website. A free Activity Worksheet is also available from the website. Activity worksheets are part of the Pearson English Readers Teacher Support Programme, which also includes Progress tests and Graded Reader Guidelines. For more information, please visit: www.pearsonenglishreaders.com

WORD LIST

account (n) a written or spoken description of something that has happened

admiral (n) a very important ship's officer

aircraft (n) a plane

cart (n) a vehicle with two or four wheels which is pulled, often by a horse

coal (n) a hard black material from under the ground that is burned to produce heat

cobalt (n) a shiny silver-white metal that can be used to make very powerful bombs

consider (v) to think very carefully about something

depend (v) a verb used to say that you cannot give a definite answer because you do not know what will happen

detect (v) to notice something that is not easy to see, hear or smell

direct (adv) without stopping or changing direction; without contacting someone else first

dirt (n) something that makes things dirty

fuel (n) something, like coal, gas or oil, that can be burned to produce heat or power

instruction (n) information or advice that tells you how to do something

Lieutenant-Commander (n) a very important ship's officer

living quarters (n) a place where a group of people live – for example, in the army

loud hailer (n) a piece of equipment that you speak through to make your voice louder

mine (n) a deep hole in the ground from which gold or coal, for example, are dug; a **minefield** is an area of land or sea where hidden bombs have been placed

navy (n) the people and ships that a country has for fighting a war at sea

nod (v) to move your head up and down to show that you understand or agree with someone